KEEPING CUSTOMERS HAPPY

DATE DUE

BRODART   Cat. No. 23-221

KEEPING CUSTOMERS HAPPY

Strategies for success

Jacqueline Dunckel
Brian Taylor

Self-Counsel Press
(a division of)
International Self-Counsel Press Ltd.
Canada   U.S.A.

Printed in Canada

First edition: November, 1988
Second edition: November, 1990; Reprinted: May, 1991

Canadian Cataloguing in Publication Data

Dunckel, Jacqueline, 1930-
    Keeping customers happy

    (Self-counsel business series)

    Previously published as: The business guide to profitable customer relations.

    ISBN 0-88908-887-X

    1. Customer relations. I. Taylor, Brian, 1931- II. Title. III. Title: The business guide to profitable customer relations. IV. Series.
HF5415.5.D85 1990   658.8'12   C90-091527-7

Self-Counsel Press
(*a division of*)
International Self-Counsel Press Ltd.
Head and Editorial Office
1481 Charlotte Road
North Vancouver, British Columbia, V7J 1H1

U.S.Address
1704 N. State Street
Bellingham, Washington 98225

CONTENTS

LIST OF FIGURES

LIST OF SAMPLES

INTRODUCTION

This is a down-to-earth book. There is no learned treatise within — just clear and effective talk on why businesses that ignore customer relations do so at their peril.

We'll discuss how successful major organizations devote considerable resources to reading public attitudes and perceptions, *why* they believe a customer relations strategy is a crucial part of their business strategy, *what* they see as the benefits, *where* and *when* they build customer service into their planning process, and *how* you can do the same for your business — large or small.

We'll talk about three questions and the answers that could keep you in business. The first: What is "bad" customer relations? The second: What is "good" customer relations? And the third question: How can I improve the current customer relations of my business?

You'll also find in the following pages plans and programs that have worked successfully for others. With a little bit of ingenuity and adaptation, they could work equally well for you or your organization.

If you're serious about beefing up the bottom line of your business, then the advice in this book will get you headed in the right direction and keep you on target. More important, you will understand why customer service is moving up the priority list in dynamic companies and why it is consuming more of their time and budget.

So let's start with a brief survey. Ask people why they patronize a particular business or retail store and chances are that they will say it's because that business has a good product, good service, convenient location, or any one of a variety of complimentary comments. Chances are also good they will *not* say it's because that business practices good customer relations.

It's ironic that when an establishment is recognized as outstanding in the business community, seldom do we think that the image it projects is planned. Yet very few organizations enjoy a favorable image by luck. Public goodwill comes from a good performance that is sensibly planned, carefully executed, and publicly acknowledged. It is earned, not bestowed.

In the past, it was common for someone in business to think, If I'm good at my business, providing good service and quality products, I'll be successful. Word will automatically spread. Well, perhaps it may spread — but probably not far enough or fast enough to keep up with the changing tastes and preferences of today's society.

Granted, you need good service and quality products to first attract the customers. But you must retain their interest to maintain your relationship. You do this by letting them know you care. While you let them know the material benefits they gain from you are substantial, you must also, psychologically and subliminally, let them know you recognize them as an important and worthwhile part of your business. People crave recognition. Cater to that need and you will be successful. Consider your clients and customers as part of your extended family.

Equally important is letting potential clients and future customers know that they, too, can become a part of your "family" and receive the same courtesy and consideration, in addition to the same dedicated services, you afford your present clientele.

Now, much of this may sound familiar, particularly if you've been involved in public relations or community relations, and much of it is similar — particularly the guiding principles. But differences may arise in the methods of implementing plans or programs.

Using the prerogative of artistic license, we've drawn a parallel between customer service and public relations by substituting "customer service" for "public relations" in this quotation attributed to *Fortune Magazine*: "Good [customer service] is good performance — publicly appreciated."

Doesn't that sentence sum up the essence of what customer service is all about? While it may seem self-evident to spread the word about your good deeds, too often people let opportunity dribble through their fingers. You must make the most of each opportunity, seizing it as though it were your last, and exploiting it to its fullest advantage.

In the *Fortune Magazine* quotation, "good performance" comes before "publicly appreciated." This is no accident of the pen. You cannot expect clients or customers to thank you or express appreciation for something they haven't yet received, no matter how noble your intent or glittering the promise.

All the exotic plans, goals, and objectives in the world don't mean a thing while they remain as plans, goals, and objectives. It is when you put them into practice that they begin to have relevance and meaning.

Many businesses have foundered on the rocks of procrastination — despite thoughtful planning and meticulous strategy — because the plans remained on paper. Nobody was committed to them. This is often the pivotal point of customer service. Frequently, the commitment to transform plans and promises into reality fades under pressure of day-to-day business activity. Yet an organization without a sensible, comprehensive, and active service philosophy is living on borrowed time.

Abraham Lincoln prophesied wisely and well when he said, "With public sentiment nothing can fail; without it, nothing can succeed." Over a century ago, Lincoln recognized that public opinion, sentiment, or perception is a powerful and motivating force in society. Today, it remains just as powerful and influential in society but has also migrated into our business economy.

Wise business people accept customer service as an essential element in public opinion. It is also a powerful management tool. When used well, it returns dividends far beyond the initial outlay of funds or investment in time and energy.

Business leaders also recognize that good customer service is not an emergency response to a crisis or a stopgap measure to bolster sagging sales. It isn't something you can get into and out of as the mood grips you or as circumstances dictate. Rather it is an ongoing, credible, and planned business activity with significant support from senior management.

So what do you need to establish or enhance a customer service program in your business? Simple. You need to think about customer service. You need to fantasize, visualize, and then realize. You need to eat, drink, and sleep it. Then you need to plan it, develop it, provide it, launch it, sustain it, encourage it, and, finally, be thankful for it — because it's paying your salary. Moreover, you must sell it to your employees because it pays their salaries as well.

If you agree with what we have said so far, read on, and we will tell you what is needed to start a vigorous customer service program, plus we will tell you who should be involved, why they need to be involved, and why their cooperation is essential to your success.

1

CUSTOMER SERVICE — WHAT IT IS AND WHAT IT IS NOT

Ask most people what customer service is and they will tell you what it is not. We all have stories of long lineups, rude waiters, indifferent clerks, lost luggage, and service technicians on interminable coffee breaks.

Many can recall, with blissful nostalgia, what service used to be. Back in the forties and fifties, when labor was cheap and prices stable, your milk arrived at the door every morning at the same time. You could phone the drugstore and have a prescription delivered free of charge, often by the druggist personally. You knew your bank manager's name and the manager knew yours. When you went to fill your car with gas, you stayed in the car, the tank was filled, the windows washed, and the oil checked by a band of uniformed gas attendants. Every Saturday, you checked out the latest 45s at the music store with its individual booths where you could play the record before buying it. It was definitely an era of service.

a. WHAT IS CUSTOMER SERVICE?

So what is customer service and what happened to it? Customer service, or good customer relations, can be described as expectations:

- The expectation that a product will produce the benefits promised

- The expectation that the service will be of the standard promised

1

- The expectation that, if expectations are not met, the seller will make good on the promise

Good customer relations is a continuing, mutually satisfying contract between two economic entities.

b. THE CHANGE IN FRONTLINE STAFF

When our economy was blue-collar based and those in the service industry were in the minority, good service was more easily measured and taken for granted. A person's word was a bond, and a handshake as good as a contract. By the mid-fifties, white-collar workers in technical, managerial, and clerical jobs outnumbered blue-collar workers. Still, good customer service was expected and it was delivered. By the seventies, inflation caused businesses to slash services to keep prices down. Deregulation led to price wars and cutbacks. A good example of this occurred in the transportation systems industry, particularly in the United States. Management moved behind closed doors. It became difficult to hire frontline service workers because of labor shortages, and the attitude toward service jobs deteriorated.

Another common example of deteriorating service is the restaurant industry. Think back; when did you last meet a "waiter"? Usually, waiters are either actors "at liberty" or students working toward their MBAs. In contrast, throughout Europe there is pride in being a waiter. It is considered a profession that takes time to master, and, as a result, the service provided is generally much better than in North America.

The first step has been taken to improve service in the food and beverage industry. In 1990 in Canada, Alberta's hospitality industry introduced training, examination, and certification for food and beverage servers, wine stewards, maitre d's, bartenders, and hosts. Developed by the Alberta Tourism Council, it is the first certification program for this industry in North America. The program is intended to foster

2

pride, status, and professionalism. The result will be better and more knowledgeable service for the customer, repeat business for the restaurant, raises for graduates who are already employed, and better starting wages for those who are newly hired: the training will pay off for all involved.

The final, and very important, factor that has contributed to the decline in customer service in recent years is that human workers have been replaced with computers and the self-service concept. Today, as a result of the reduction in services and increased automation to save money, consumers find themselves doing business with frontline people who are underpaid, undertrained, and undermotivated. They are overworked to keep labor costs down and underpaid to keep product prices down. They are unmotivated because they see no future with the company. How can they develop a sense of pride if they find it difficult to experience a sense of accomplishment? Treated as the lowest people on the ladder, working in jobs that emphasize skills that require little training, they are not expected to solve the customer's problems or be creative. The frontline worker has become a human robot with no decision-making responsibility. Even the standardized greetings — "Hi, I'm Ned. I'll be serving you this evening" — and the inevitable "Have a nice day!" have no warmth, personality, or meaning.

The customer's concerns or feelings take second place at best. In most large department stores today, shopping is a jungle experience of searching through over-stocked counters and back-to-back racks. Waiting on yourself, you search for the cashier's enclave, wait in line, then wait some more as the cashier taps a multi-digit inventory code into the computer. You are lucky if you make eye contact. It is perhaps not surprising that this attitude has resulted in diminished sales for major department stores. Customers in the sixties were interested in product, in the seventies, in marketing, and in the eighties, in service, but in the nineties, customers demand **quality service** and **personal attention.** Major stores should take their cue from small businesses and give customers the individual attention they demand.

c. THE CHANGING DEMANDS OF THE CUSTOMER

Where once the customer was king, in some instances he or she now seems to be barely tolerated. "If only the customers would go away and leave me alone, I could get my work done," was heard from a travel agent. "This would be a great job if it weren't for the students," from a college admissions clerk. "These elevator managers make such demands," from a supervisor at a grain purchasing company.

In these cases, the work has become more important than the travelers seeking information, the students, and the grain buyers who are responsible in the first place for there being any work and, consequently, any pay. The machinery and the system has taken precedence. We have become obsessed with servicing the job rather than the customer.

Customers tolerated this situation for some time. Many people gave up service in hope of lower prices. For a while, everyone shopped at mega bulk stores, filled their own tires, and made lonely treks to the bank machine. But by the time the 1980s rolled around, two-income families were more common; as a result, time and schedules became more important. And now, in the 1990s, the public wants convenience plus quick, personal service. Minor inconveniences fray a customer's nerves and lead to vocal demands.

Once again, consumers are saying "help me" and meaning it. It is not a plea; it is a demand. Since 60% of North American industries are service industries, consumers now have the luxury of being able to shop around for that help, whether it be for transportation, communication, utilities, financial consultation, insurance, real estate, accounting, food, clothing, recreation, or personal needs. Consumers are returning to those companies who always knew what their

4

customers wanted or anticipated what they would want. Whenever people travel, they can be sure that McDonald's restaurants will provide the same burger, served in clean surroundings, and delivered quickly; IBM will have the "future" machine developed today; Woodwards, a western Canadian department store, really means it when it says, "The customer is always right," and the Central Coffee Shoppe in the southern U.S. town of Manning, which has had a member of the Metropole family behind the counter for over 50 years, still serves the wonderful lemon pie that kept actor Jimmy Cagney returning again and again.

d. YOUR BUSINESS AND THE FUTURE OF CUSTOMER SERVICE

Your customers in the 1990s may change with the growing number of professionals, single parents, new immigrants, and retirees. Who serves your customers may change as well as you recognize the need to instill pride in your staff, pay in accordance to their performance, and build an effective team. Customer relations is the mirror image of employee relations. If you have a high turnover of staff, you'll have a high turnover of customers. And it is just as hard to find new staff as it is to court new customers. Better to work to keep both.

You will have a distinct competitive edge going into the 1990s if you and your company or organization recognize that service — good customer relations — is not just the business of frontline employees, but the business of everyone. Everyone will have to recognize that it is a tool you have to budget for, train to use, and most important, believe in.

While each marketplace is different in size and scope, all marketplaces, all vendors and stall holders in the market, and all market frequenters operate under the principle of "presumed satisfaction," or "assumed response." For example, if you buy a can opener, you expect it to work. If not, you expect the store to give you another, return your money, or have the faulty one repaired. Today, this is the hidden message on all items in the market. Maybe you didn't put that message on your goods and services and maybe you don't believe it is there because you can't actually see it. But, rest assured, it *is* there.

It is not the message itself that can play havoc with your organization, it is your response to that implied message that can dislodge the fulcrum and upset the balance. That is what we zero in on in this book: blending the ingredients in the marketplace. Instead of rehashing all the motherhood statements about excellence that have been made over the past few years, which we presume you agree with as we do, we want to get down to some basic ideas. We believe you want techniques and suggestions for building a quality service program in your company. So let's plan it together.

2
THE "WHY" OF CUSTOMER RELATIONS

Probably the first thought that entered your mind when you picked up this book was, I hope it's not just another get better-richer-faster text that shows how to eliminate stress while hugging your boss and reducing carbohydrate intake. In other words, satisfaction in 17 seconds a day.

If that is what you are expecting, return this book to the shelf and wend your way back to your office because there is no magic in these pages. Instead, this book will focus on, and help you focus on, the reality of the marketplace. Once you accept that the market is the great determinant, the fulcrum on which your entire future pivots, then you can get down to the business of good business, which is servicing the people with whom you would like to do business.

a. THE 90-SECOND TEST

Before you saddle up and ride off in all directions, ask yourself three very basic questions about improvement in service excellence and about your organization. Allow yourself 30 seconds to answer each question.

(a) Why us? (What do we stand to gain?)

(b) Why now? (What could we gain from a delay?)

(c) Why bother? (What do we stand to lose?)

These are excellent questions to kick off your mental process.

When a customer walks into a store, the products are attractively packaged and the ribbon and tinsel tend to draw eyes away from the unobtrusive security tag that represents

7

expectations. The department store expects people to pay for their selections. From experience, they know that some people will not, so they have a security system. When someone walks through the exit without paying for an item, ringing alarms announce the oversight to everyone within five blocks. In this way, the store knows that someone is failing to meet expectations.

Business is much the same. All actions come with expectation tags and customers expect businesses to fulfill those expectations. How well business people respond to customer expectations determines how long they remain in business. If the expectations are met, the customer's alarm stays silent. If not, the alarm rings out and the customer is warned that this business should be avoided in future. Unfortunately, the customer's alarm, unlike a security alarm, is inaudible to you. You will never know why that customer doesn't return, but you will count the loss in your ledger. So, make sure you never let a customer go away with that ringing in the ears by always meeting customer expectations.

1. Why us?

As you think about why you should implement a customer relations plan, keep in mind that whether you know it or not, you already have a program in place. It may be informal or invisible, but it definitely says something about your business.

You really don't have to decide whether to have a program or not. The only decision is whether your program will build and support positive customer relations or whether you'll allow customer relationships to lurch along as best they can. It really is no choice. Since you have a customer relations program in place, then surely it makes sense to enhance it. Make it work for you.

Why should you invest time and training in customer relations? Let's look at what you and your organization stand to gain. First, our population is becoming consumer oriented at an earlier age than ever before. It seems that coincident with the ability to walk and talk is the ability to say "candy" and "cookie." Kids know what they want and know how to get it (an important thought to tuck away at the back of your mind as today's children become tomorrow's customers).

Television plays a role in this, of course. Children's programs are an ideal vehicle for promoting products and encouraging buying habits. And here's the interesting or sad part (depending whether you are a retailer or a parent): children's purchases now require more than just spare change. Nickel and dime candies have been replaced by monster candy bars, and the once-a-week trip to the candy store has become an everyday event for some young people.

The point is, people are being conditioned to buy at an earlier age, and the amounts they spend are increasing substantially.

Second, we are consumers for longer. As fast as labor-saving devices are developed to help people set aside more time for themselves, all manner of recreational products are developed to show them how to use the time saved. The outcome is that people are healthier and living longer. Significantly, those enjoying the "golden years" still need to be supplied with more of what they've been using ... more autos, more appliances, more food, more clothes, you name it.

Now, tie the two thoughts together: people are becoming consumers at an earlier age, and current consumers are enjoying extended life spans. What you have, in effect, is an enlarging market.

Third, consumers are more sophisticated. They not only have more disposable income (and seem more inclined to dispose of it than either their parents or grandparents), but they are better educated, more informed, have higher expectations, and are aware of their rights and options in the marketplace. More significantly, they are not hesitant to exercise those rights and options. They become vocal when necessary. This awareness can be a blessing or a curse. Today's consumers can be staunch allies, or formidable foes. Wise business people will get them on side.

What do these consumers want? Very simply what they have always wanted but rarely received — quality goods and quality service. The difference is that today's consumer is in the driver's seat, with enough muscle to dictate business terms and the money to pay for choices.

The last few years have seen a consumer revolt against inferior products and slipshod service. People feel they are entitled to quality products delivered in a quality manner. Enlightened companies have responded to the new wave of consumerism, and this is good news for everybody, because sellers and buyers in every business are also consumers. When progressive companies force other companies to improve their practices, we all benefit. And, of course, companies that respond to consumer demand are laying a foundation for business longevity. Even consumers for whom cost is a high priority demand that items look good, perform well, and last a long time. They don't see this as an unreasonable demand. What they are really saying is, Give us the best of both worlds.

As a businessperson you have to decide how to respond to this demand. You can try to switch your customers from quality to cost or vice versa; you can just ignore their demands (and look forward to declining sales); or you can respond to their needs by offering top quality at fair prices backed with superlative service. Can that actually be done? Is it possible? Many companies are proving that it is not only possible, it is downright profitable. It is also downright crucial.

Surveys show that about 70% of all people who enter retail outlets are never even acknowledged. They probably never go back. For all intents and purposes they were never even there. They were in your store or office, and were obviously interested in parting with some of their cash. But you wouldn't let them. Even worse, you let them know you didn't care and weren't interested in having them back. What a tragedy.

A further sobering thought: of those who do stay, and are dissatisfied with their experience, 97% of them will never complain. They won't volunteer the information, and unless you assist them to complain, you will miss the vital feedback.

If people are becoming more vocal, yet there is still a whopping 97% who won't tell you when your service is failing, this suggests a vast army of unhappy customers out there looking for alternative suppliers. Perhaps some of the disillusioned were once your customers. Perhaps many others could become your customers if you offered products or services that were just slightly better than those of your competitors.

The point is this: if you lose customers it's because you choose to do so.

The salvation is this: you can also choose to keep customers by committing yourself to a customer relations program.

One word of warning: some people think in terms of the "quick fix" as a substitute for service excellence and our advice is, Don't do it! In the long run, it won't work, and it often doesn't work in the short term, either.

Temporary patch jobs, while they take on an air of permanence, never get better because they are built on a makeshift foundation. An ad hoc solution may get an angry client off the phone or off your back, but the phone will certainly ring again when the "patch" peels off.

Some companies grasp for the quick fix and plan to initiate programs of good customer relations and service excellence when times get better and finances aren't so tight. But it is essential to accept that service excellence isn't a "good times" or even a part-time exercise. It must be a continual and consistent process. The old adage "An ounce of prevention is worth a pound of cure," is still true today. You have to make the time available to implement a permanent customer relations program because it is becoming increasingly evident that satisfying the expectations for quality in products and services is the key to survival for many businesses.

You *can* keep customers happy, *and* keep them coming back, but you cannot leave it to chance. Plan a customer relations program, design it, develop it, refine it, practice it, announce it, and then support it 100%.

By now you are probably asking yourself if it is worth the effort. Maybe it seems like a lot of energy to expend. But remember, you are in the business of attracting people to your product, service, or location. The competition is attempting to do the same. In order to do it better than they do, or be more effective or successful, you have to plan your strategy, train your employees, and continually practice good business skills. Above everything else, you must become committed to the idea that good relations with your customers is an ongoing affair.

Rest assured the opposition is doing the same. When one of you comes out ahead, it is usually because of better planning, or better execution, or better customer relations. Perhaps a combination of all three.

Why not swing the odds in your favor? You can boost your own effectiveness and that of your organization with policies and procedures that are designed for the benefit of the customer. Customers are quick to recognize this.

When you ask, Why us? you are really asking, Do I want to stay in business? If you are reluctant to get involved with customer relations, you are handing the advantage to your competition on a platter. Doesn't it make better sense to ask, Why *not* us?

2. Why now?

The second question, Why now? is harder to answer. Who really knows when an appropriate time really is appropriate? Like most business decisions, the answer to this question is based on informed intuition. But here is a rule of thumb for customer relations: if you don't have a formal program in place, in the works, or in the back of your mind, the best time for you and your company is right now!

There are two major reasons. One, it is essential for survival. Two, there's money to be made giving people what they want. Either option is reason enough to get excited, but together, we're talking business nirvana. And who isn't looking for a little bit of business heaven?

Some companies are candidates for disaster. They are so wrapped up in the daily business routine that they forget that business works *for customers*. They exhaust their energies trying to do the job right before considering whether they are doing the right job. Some may be aware they are in a precarious position, others may be oblivious to the fact, but for all of them, survival is the name of the game. After all, the main function of all businesses should be to be in business tomorrow. The key, for many companies, will be good customer relations.

What are the hurdles to kicking off a customer relations program today? Probably the biggest obstacle is you! And here's why.

Almost any attempt to motivate ourselves and others runs headlong into the human scourge — procrastination. It is easier to look for reasons not to do something than to get on with doing it. Have you ever been guilty of using such phrases as, Why don't we wait for just a little longer, the market may improve next week? I'll have more time, I'm swamped now, and, It just wouldn't work here? Even worse, Let's study it more. These are all ways of putting things off.

Well, delaying a customer relations program is a sure recipe for disaster. The way you treat your customers will make or break you. It is that simple.

Equally simple is the solution: Do something about it. Don't sit on your hands. Of course it is easier said than done, but the crucial element in any customer relations program is to get going, to start today.

So the call is for action, and action today.

Even if you've had a program running for several years, this could be a good time to re-evaluate your original objectives and see if they are still valid. Do they still hold up in the light of rapidly changing business operations and values? Has time burnished them, or tarnished them? Maybe this is an opportune time for re-dedication to the principles of good customer relations — rather like renewing marriage vows.

If you need further proof of the need to start now, just consider the time lag between cause and effect at your place of business. By the time questions trickle down and answers filter back up many sunrises will have passed.

That same lag applies to customer belief. Just because you *say* you give good service doesn't make it so. A reputation for service excellence must be nurtured. It's much like planting a seed that has to germinate, take root, grow, and blossom to fulfil its destiny. And it sure helps if it gets some tender loving care. But successful gardeners know that before any of this can take place the seed bed — the growing medium — has to be prepared. In the same way, members of your staff have to be "prepared" to accept the ideas and the policies, if a customer relations program is to have any chance of success.

An effective program will not burst into bloom overnight. Many elaborate plans have foundered because of unrealistic time lines for launching or enhancing a program. In essence, introducing a new program or integrating changes in an existing program requires changes to an organization's culture, and that takes time. In fact you may have to overcome some ingrained skepticism about what you are promising and what you are delivering. And that skepticism may be just as strong in-house as it is with the general public.

The key is to avoid self-righteous proclamations about the great service you offer. If you fail to provide it, nothing will destroy your credibility faster. Before you tell people about improvements in service, make sure there are improvements worth talking about. Once the improvements have been shown to work, and your staff is achieving service excellence consistently, then, and only then, tell people. Let the actions speak for themselves. Rest assured, people recognize good service and remember it. They make mental notes about the good, the bad, and the ugly and those memories influence their buying decisions down the road.

Start immediately, get your staff involved, get them excited and enthused, and lead by example.

3.   Why bother?

Why bother? is a key question, and should be asked more often about everything you do in business.

In the case of customer relations you bother because there is no choice. As we pointed out in a previous chapter, if you wish to remain in business or keep your present job, then you *have* to get involved. And the sooner the better, because businesses today don't have the luxury of unlimited time.

We also mentioned earlier that the expectations of our society are changing substantially. Every area in which human beings operate today comes under public scrutiny — not a casual glance but intensive investigation in a public forum. Business and industry are being challenged as never before and respected business leaders familiar with their traditional roles and comfortable with corporate activities now find themselves thrust into the spotlight. Under that intensive glare they must defend corporate policies and actions. Many find this difficult to handle as time-honoured standards are challenged by questioning consumers. The transition from, We know what's best for you, to, Here's what we're planning, and We would like your opinion, has meant rethinking corporate strategy.

It is easy to understand why bewildered people lash out at the nearest target — the corporation. Quickly evolving scientific and technological breakthroughs are increasing complexity in an already complex life. And there are plenty of people out there who have been mistreated, ignored, insulted, and foisted off with inferior products for far too long. They are waiting for just the right opportunity to hit back. When they do this, it becomes a matter of principle that they oppose your plans because they've learned to distrust you.

That's why you need to develop a sense of urgency about your customer relations activities. You need to start now. Your efforts needn't be complicated or sophisticated to begin with, just built on common sense and your awareness of how you would like to be treated.

Here's a simple way to begin. On a plain writing pad jot down the names of your competitors and the customer relations activities you believe each of them practices. List all the activities you think they do well, then list the activities you think they do poorly.

Now put the pad in a drawer for three months. At the end of the three months, review what you have written. Were your choices realistic, were you correct in your assumptions, have they changed any of their practices, or have they added any others?

If you repeat this review each quarter, by the end of next year you will be able to look back at which competitors are still in business and decide whether customer relations played a significant part in their survival. The list will also help you differentiate between those just hanging on and those flourishing and prospering. You may also be able to decide whether the demise of some competitors was attributable to poor customer relations, poor planning, or poor execution. In any case, you will have a record of what works and what doesn't in your market. You will be able to use this personal case study to avoid making the same mistakes.

The advantage of your competitor list is that as an observer you can learn what the successful companies did and consider adapting their programs or activities to suit your organization. In other words, don't re-invent the wheel, but make the wheel fit your vehicle ... in this case your company.

We say throughout the book that the people and companies who are in business for the long haul view customer relations as a management tool. It's another skill, another technique, another business activity aimed at satisfying customers so the organization can be profitable. After all, without profit there is no rationale for the organization.

But there can also be a downside to the search for profit. A growing number of organizations strive for short-term financial gains to placate a jittery market or soothe shareholder concern. Controllers or chief financial officers face fierce competition, declining productivity, and the threat of an inflationary economy. As they juggle mounting costs, they keep their eyes fixed firmly on the next quarterly or annual report. That's their job.

Unfortunately, some do it too stringently. The result can be that programs not readily perceived as adding to today's bottom line are put on hold, shuffled aside, or left to drift or manage as best they can.

In effect, management is saying, We want results now, and we'll think about tomorrow when tomorrow comes. It's almost as if they are demanding interest in their bank account before they have made a deposit.

That attitude can quickly spread throughout an organization. Keeping the lid on costs becomes the reason for trimming all activities that don't provide an obvious boost to profits. In fact overzealous trimming can become endemic and end up entrenched in the company's mission statement.

Unfortunately for those given the responsibility of managing the customer relations function, most service-oriented programs tend to provide returns over the longer haul. Goodwill takes time to accumulate. More significantly, the benefits are hard to explain to financial managers bent on survival at all costs.

When a customer relations program is ignored or deliberately disregarded, management commitment and employee response erode in tandem. Even worse, when a program that has been painstakingly assembled is abandoned, an atmosphere of distrust develops, creating deep-rooted misgivings about getting involved in the future. A program cannot be turned on and off like a spigot.

Other factors affect management mind-set about taking care of customers, too. Changes in the way business conducts business, or changes in the growing technology of the business, can have profound implications. Often we turn to technology to solve problems, or to improve productivity or efficiency, but in the race for streamlining, sometimes we alienate the very audience we are trying to capture or retain. How many times have you heard, I could tolerate this job if there were fewer interruptions. There's a wealth of information in that terse message if you take the time to listen.

Ask yourself the basic question, Will we ever reach the stage where customer contact will disappear? Obviously the answer is no. Not as obvious is evidence that as we automate in one area we find a corresponding need to humanize in another.

The giant food warehouses are a good example. They originally boasted of great savings because of minimum frills. Frequently located away from the main shopping area, or near an industrial zone, they usually consisted of plain walls, basic steel shelving, and pack-it-yourself service.

Yes, they did save customers money, and name brand products were available in copious quantities, but when the cost factor became the only criterion, people once again sought out convenience and service. Food industry competitors, recognizing the growing disenchantment, saw an opportunity. They seized the moment and fought back with carry-out service, refurbished stores, and staff trained to make the customers feel welcome and important.

The response of lower price retailers was to renovate their "warehouses" into people places again. They recognized that in a market with considerable choice people will gravitate to pleasant warm surroundings and, more significantly, to pleasant warm people who seem interested in the problems and well-being of their customers. What we see now, of course, is a galaxy of stores offering varying combinations of savings and service, with each one carefully monitoring the others.

In the seventies, the single-minded drive for efficiency at the cost of customer comfort encouraged the emergence of stores that catered particularly to the human need to be acknowledged as an individual. Boutiques flourished based on personal contact and conversation. They were places that not only recognized a name or a face, but more important, recognized the need for human contact in an increasingly sterile world. Boutiques offered acceptance and in the process cultivated their customers' self-esteem.

The lesson for business is that customer demands for efficiency, economy, and savings go hand in hand with a hidden plea for the human voice and the definite human touch. An impersonal customer approach will have limited success today, but taking a people approach that ignores proven technological advances will let the advantage of speed and efficiency move to the competition. There has to be a marriage of technology/systems and human values. Some may see this as a contradiction, but to perceptive business operators it suggests an opportunity to give customers what they tell us they want.

Some organizations have seen this surge in consumerism as an opportunity to stay in the race — to survive and perhaps even prosper — and they've grasped it. They have used technology to take much of the drudgery and repetition out of routine tasks and encouraged their employees to come up with innovative ideas to improve efficiency. Energy and effort is focussed instead on the point where the company and the customer come face to face.

It is at this point that businesses find the real payoff. As quality becomes a password in any given industry, there are fewer ways to differentiate products. For example, one appliance becomes much like another, except for the number of buttons or the color.

The benefits for the customer must therefore come from the expectations of clearly superior service, both before and after the sale. What the customer is looking for, and what alert companies will provide, is "satisfaction." And satisfaction can be measured at the cash register.

So the question, Why bother? is really redundant. If you wish to stay in business, you will bother. Those who don't, simply won't survive. And it may be a lingering death.

If you choose not to bother, be prepared to meet a number of consumers only too willing to tackle the "Goliaths" in business and industry. The advantage is now swinging to the small guy who faces overwhelming odds in money and materials to fight the battles.

Poor "David" gains the sympathy of the public, frequently the politicians, and sometimes the judiciary, who more and more are examining the issue of "expectations."

If you're wondering where the Davids of the world are gaining victories, look no further than your local newspaper. You'll see articles demanding changes in your local hospital, the police force, the transit system, city hall, school boards — you name it, and it's probably in there, or will be soon.

While many of these battles may appear insignificant, they usually involve the right to know, the right to be informed, the right of common sense. People are no longer prepared to be bamboozled by technical details or patronized into accepting what they don't understand.

For example, the small print in legal documents or insurance policies is being questioned more frequently. People are casting a jaundiced eye at the *whereases* and *heretofores*, seeing them as an escape route for business if the going gets sticky. Consensus is that these documents leave a reader befuddled and in need of a lawyer to interpret both meaning and intent.

What's the point we wish to make? The individual is gaining more power, or at least is exercising the power that he or she already has, whether actual or implied.

These changes in our society provide challenges that the astute business operator will interpret as opportunities, excellent opportunities for growth and ultimately profit.

Good customer relations pays off inside the business too. It fosters loyalty, encourages productivity, builds self-esteem, and develops pride in accomplishment. A bonus is that it attracts the capable people you need to operate successfully, which in turn creates respect and goodwill with clients, customers, suppliers, agencies, and within the community.

Effective customer relations creates a continuing demand for your organization's services, which means business can grow, and so can you as an individual.

b. CAN IT WORK FOR YOU?

While we use the term survival to describe the reasons for customer service, perhaps it is more palatable to think of it as "enlightened self-interest." And if you are talking about self-interest, doesn't it make sense to become involved in your own destiny? You can no longer leave your future to chance, or to the "I'll get around to it" philosophy of an individual who has been "volunteered" to develop and implement the program and who may already be swamped with major responsibilities.

Just as you have your personal priorities, so, too, must your business. We believe that if survival is part of your company's plans for the future, then quality, service, and excellence need to be boosted higher on the list of priorities.

Can it be done? Most certainly. It starts with commitment — to yourself, to your company, and to your plan. You need to become committed to setting standards, designing a strategy, developing plans, and then implementing them. These are the four simple but crucial steps to survival in today's business market.

c. CHECKING OUT ATTITUDES

Next time you are in a store, try this simple exercise. It may reinforce an attitude you have about the store, or it may change your attitude entirely.

Choose an item in the store, and then ask a clerk if it is available in another color, style, or model. If so, ask how much it would cost, and how long before it would come in.

Then see how much time the clerk is willing to devote to answering your questions and making you feel your request is important. Does the clerk respond well to you? Does he or she display an attitude of interest, of caring about satisfying you? Is he or she courteous, diplomatic, and anxious to please?

This same scenario is played out daily around the world in literally billions of transactions, and each one is an opportunity to improve or cement a relationship, each one is a chance to ensure survival. Make a commitment to grasp all of those opportunities for your company. Do you know how your customers are treated by your staff? Do you encourage good customer relations?

d. THE KEY WORD IS IMPROVEMENT

We said earlier there is no magic solution in this book that can make problems evaporate, and as a business person you already know that. You are probably skeptical about getting richer-better-faster for some very good reasons.

But we do have to emphasize that getting better is central to any strategy for improving quality and service. It is fundamental to business and industry as well as to the individual because there is a built-in need to improve; it's part of our nature — our psyche. We are all born strivers and achievers, whether we like it or not. Where we differ is the level of achievement we are satisfied with, and that depends on the goals we set for ourselves and the goals we expect to accomplish.

Trying to get better also allows you to look back at former accomplishments, gauge your improvement, and set higher and more demanding benchmarks of satisfaction. This is what happened at the ABC Shoppe, the store in the case study that is examined at the end of each section of this book. By following this case study, you will experience first hand the procedures we suggest in this book that can then be transferred to your own company or situation.

CASE STUDY: THE ABC SHOPPE — A GIFT BOUTIQUE FOR MEN AND WOMEN

After careful market research, a freelance writer, John, and a dentist, Mary, have opened a specialty boutique that sells upgrade accessories for men and women. They are adequately financed and located in a trendy area near other stores of equal quality. Their stock features shirts, blouses, ties, socks, sweaters, scarves, jewelry, and travel and gift items.

John is able to give more time to the store, so he has assumed the role of manager. Mary, who has an active dental practice, takes over the bookkeeping and buying chores. She travels a great deal, which makes it possible for her to visit markets and make personal selections for the store.

John and Mary have hired three sales people to work overlapping shifts, evenings and part time:

(a) April has previous experience in sales in a home accessory store.

(b) June is a university student whose previous experience has been with McDonald's and as a camp counselor.

(c) Jim is a retired accountant.

After six months in business, John and Mary have concluded that while their advertising is attracting customers, the customers do not return after the initial visit. Sales have remained constant, but without repeat customers this could easily change. John and Mary decide they need to develop a customer relations program that will assure them a strong customer base. They are enthusiastic, willing to take part, and will accept criticism and new ideas.

Now, follow this case study as you read the remaining chapters of this book. You'll see how John and Mary were able to solve their problems and put an effective customer service program into place; and you'll see how the same ideas can work for you and your business.

3

WHAT DOES THE CUSTOMER EXPECT AND WHY?

Shopper laments lack of service

I have decided not to purchase clothes until I can find a store willing to serve me. Today I went shopping for a new outfit at a large women's store and was totally ignored.

There were three sales people and my husband and I. Service? Ha! Ha! I tried on the outfit, came out, and they still acted as if I were not there.

I'm not going to spend hundreds of dollars without some service. Needless to say, they lost the sale and any hope of future sales.

(Letter to the Editor
The Toronto Star
Sunday, January 21, 1990)

This letter answers the question for us. The writer had an objective: to buy. She was not "just looking." She had money to spend. She wanted *attention*. She was ignored.

Customers want quality products and service, and more! They want to be treated with special care, to be made to feel important, no matter what the size of the purchase. They want to feel confident that the seller will be there for them if anything goes wrong.

Spending money, whether for a chocolate bar or a home, takes a decision on the part of the buyer. The decision may be impulsive or well thought out. No matter. Your customers expect acknowledgment and attention. They have made a decision to spend money. They want acknowledgment for that decision and attention for making the choice to buy from you. When you consider the amount of money a satisfied, loyal customer can bring to your business over a period of years, then the minutes you spend with that customer take on new meaning and value. In five years, a satisfied customer spends $22,000 at the supermarket, in twenty years $3,000 in appliances, and during a lifetime $142,000 on automobiles.

Not all service has to do with money and goods. We were interviewed recently on a television program. Advised to arrive at a designated time we followed our own advice on good business etiquette and arrived ten minutes early. The receptionist greeted us with, "You're too early. The producer is still at lunch. Sit over there." Her exact words! Now, appearing on a TV show is not our everyday activity. Already nervous, we did as we were told. Our confidence was further eroded after she sent us to makeup. While sitting under the all-seeing eye of the makeup artist, we were further challenged by the producer who roared in saying, "So here you are. We've been looking all over for you. Telephoned your office. We didn't know you were in the building." The receptionist had failed to announce our arrival and whereabouts. The result was a nervous producer and crew, a testy interviewer, and edgy guests — which did not produce a good product for the viewer.

In a world where loneliness and low self-esteem are major talk show problems, customers with money to spend want to be made to feel special. You need to meet their social needs, their need for self-worth, and their need to achieve in a highly competitive world. Customers want you to treat them with honesty and integrity. Be sure you are honest and sincere in what you say when building self-esteem. Women are getting wary of sales clerks who compliment them on what they are wearing, an obvious reference to their good taste, when they are dressed in a back-of-the-closet reject.

Customers want you to have a sense of trust and loyalty for them. They in turn will have some for you. Loyalty to a business brings customers back again and again. Loyalty makes customers recommend you to others. You want to build an organization that makes customers want to do business with you. Customers expect your employees to find what they want, need, and expect. If you don't make spending money a personal, special event they will stop buying and go elsewhere. (This applies to company buying as well. Companies don't buy. Individuals buy for companies.) It is ridiculous to spend large amounts of money to get customers back who would never have left if they had been treated properly.

a. CUSTOMERS EXPECT TO BE TREATED LIKE GUESTS

When you invite guests to your home you make preparations to please them. You choose food, music, and entertainment you know they will enjoy. You spruce up and put on your party face and manners. The business that sets the best example of treating customers like guests is Disney. At Disneyland and Disney World customers are called guests and showered with attention and, yes, love. Customers, like guests, expect the following:

(a) They expect clean, comfortable, attractive, unintimidating surroundings.

(b) They expect to be welcomed by someone who smiles. Sadly, only 50% to 60% of all frontline people smile at their customers. Smiles welcome and relax both customer and employee.

28

Some businesses know the value of a smile and actually promote smiles as part of their service. In a recent Canada Trust ad, the copy read: *Canada Trust people are friendly. And helpful. We like to smile, and we call our customers by name. And, of course, we say "thanks."*

(c) They expect to talk to someone who looks professional and is well groomed. The service garage that gets our business is the one that supplies their mechanics with clean coveralls every day, lays down work mats, and washes the car before returning it.

(d) They expect immediate attention. You greet your guests at the door and don't leave them unattended. Neither should you neglect your customers.

(e) They expect you to make strong eye contact with them. In our culture, eye contact acknowledges people's existence and conveys your interest in them. Think of how many times you felt non-existent while trying to make eye contact with a waiter!

(f) They expect to be addressed by names that are spelled correctly and properly pronounced. Names are personal identification. Once you have obtained a customer's name, use it judiciously, and err on the side of formality — Mr., Mrs., Ms., until they indicate otherwise.

They expect to be listened to. Really *heard* by someone who cares. You listen intently to your guests and make sure their needs are attended to, so you should do the same with customers.

(g) They expect not just words of reassurance but action behind the words. When our Toyota dealership did not have a part for our car clock they assured us it would be in within the week. Six days later they called apologizing because the part had not arrived.

Four days later they called to let us know the part was in and could be installed at our convenience. We hadn't been concerned, for the car ran without the clock, but their concern strengthened our loyalty to them.

(h) They expect to be served by people who know all about the business or they lose confidence. Employees need to learn to say, "I don't have the answer right here. I'll get the information for you and get back to you immediately."

(i) They expect confidentiality. Guests don't expect their party conversation to be repeated throughout the neighborhood. Similarly your customers expect you to treat their business transactions confidentially.

A well-known Seattle business woman selected a bridal dress several months before she intended to announce her marriage. Her plans changed abruptly when news of her purchase was broadcast around the city by a boutique employee (who was fired for her indiscretion).

(j) They expect you to be charming, hospitable, caring, and always in a good mood even when they are brusque, rude, and complaining. All of us have entertained an obnoxious guest at some time, yet remained charming hosts or hostesses to the bitter end of the evening.

(k) They expect surprises. Pleasant surprises! Guests love party favors, balloons, place cards, and take-home gifts. Customers like the chocolates on the pillow, the newspaper at the door, the rose in the restaurant, the note or follow-up call after making a purchase.

The Broadmoor Hotel in Colorado Springs, Colorado, does all of these things beautifully. A box of chocolates awaits you in your room with a gold engraved card from the manager, the bed is turned down in the evening, and soft music is playing. Ladies receive a long-stemmed rose when they enter the dining room. And there's a vase on the table to keep it fresh until you leave! The Holiday Inn in Sarnia, Ontario, writes you a letter after your return home. In our case the manager personalized it by apologizing for the weather which had been less than friendly when we were there and promising better the next time we stayed. In the same city, The Brass Lantern antique store carefully wrapped some dishes for us. The father of the manager fashioned an ingenious handle for the box so it could be carried on to the plane.

How do you find, keep, and develop staff who will "go the extra mile"? You want to build a team of employees who are not doing "just a job" but are taking a step along their career paths. To motivate employees you must offer them —

(a) challenging work;

(b) salaries that recognize the contribution their effort makes to the overall success of the business;

(c) input into decision making, whether it is toward company policy, work scheduling, hiring, or customer relations;

(d) opportunities to learn and advance; and

(e) praise, recognition, and rewards.

As we mentioned at the outset, many frontline people are poorly paid and without power to make customer-related decisions. When you change those conditions you will have dedicated employees who will stay in their jobs longer and contribute more.

b. CUSTOMERS EXPECT ATTENTION

Most customers are well educated. Many are professionals, well trained and skilled. Excelling in their own jobs, they give attention to detail and expect the same from others. They want to do business with people who will do the following:

(a) Give, not just service, but *quality* service.

(b) Make quality service a *habit*, not just a slogan. Well-run businesses know that behavior must be consistent with slogans and all other advertising.

(c) Go the extra mile: get it delivered today, shortened by tomorrow, changed in minutes. We purchased car windshield wipers at Canadian Tire intending to install them ourselves. None of our screwdrivers worked to remove the old blades. When we returned to Canadian Tire to ask what kind we should be using, an employee demonstrated by changing the wipers at no cost. He went the extra mile.

(d) Solve problems now. Nothing is more maddening to customers than to realize their problems cannot be solved by the person at the counter. Worse is to be sent on a telephone treasure hunt for the solution. Customers want frontline people to have authority to think and act for themselves.

(e) Have strong recovery skills when you are at fault; apologize if necessary. Admit your mistake, then move to correct it: "I'm sorry this happened. Let me see what I can do to correct this mistake." Make no excuses, then go the extra mile. Give them the unexpected: a dozen roses in the room they were promised at two that was not ready until four. Grumbling students waiting in long, hot registration lines at a college received unexpected cold soda pop. They soon forgot administration had miscalculated the time it would take to process each student.

c. CUSTOMERS EXPECT TO BE PART OF YOUR SERVICE

When you build a loyal customer base you create a partnership or family. Family members or partners like to have a say in what goes on. By having that say, they commit themselves to ownership and loyalty. Here are some ways to get your customers committed to being part of your service.

1. Ask them!

Ask them to comment on your service in one of the following ways:

(a) Verbally, at point of purchase. This happens often in restaurants. ("Was everything to your satisfaction?")

(b) On report cards. These are found in hotels and restaurants. They may be filled out on the premises or mailed back. If the latter, they should be in the form of a prepaid post card.

(c) Random phone calls to known customers. Phone at convenient times. Have short, predetermined questions ready. Make the calls yourself. This gives them importance. Send a note later thanking them for their input.

(d) If your business is large, select a focus group for a phone survey which may be conducted by an outside source or staff member. Be sure you okay the people to be called, the questions, and the procedure. After all, these calls are part of your business image.

(e) If yours is a business that goes beyond provincial or state boundaries, you can have a toll-free number for your customers to call in complaints and compliments. Let them know in your mail-out that you want to hear from them. This is particularly good if you have a mail-order catalogue business. But whatever your business, all your customers should know that you want them to tell you when something is wrong because you will make it right. When things are right you want your customers to tell *other* people! One company pulled a whole shipment of jam off the shelves when a long-standing customer called to tell them the labels were either on crooked or upside down.

2. Let your customers be a part of your reward system

Forms that customers fill out and give to employees can be used as part of your employee recognition evaluation. This gives your customers the opportunity to be part of your business. A satisfied customer wants to thank or praise the clerk, the bank teller, or mechanic who went the extra mile. The form gives them that opportunity. Points can be given for cards received. They can have titles like "Good Going!" "Thanks a Bunch!" (flower motif), "Your Gold Star" (just like kindergarten!), "Merit Badge." (See Sample #1.)

3. Establish a customer advisory council

Good customers can come up with good ideas on how to improve products and service. They know what they want and how they want it. They can also test products and services for you. General Motors called five customers every three months for five years on their Fiero model. From their customer comments it was discovered that the front windshield cracked and they were able to correct the fault while still in production.

d. CUSTOMERS EXPECT THE SYSTEM TO WORK FOR THEM, NOT AGAINST THEM

How many times have you been told: "It can't be done because of company policy," "We don't do it that way," "Our computer isn't set to take that information," "You'll have to wait until Monday. Joe handles that and he's off for the week." We could go on and on. When a system forces the customer to conform or learn the system, then it is not meet-

SAMPLE #1
EMPLOYEE MERIT REPORT

**DID YOU GET SUPERIOR SERVICE
FROM ONE OF OUR STAFF?**

We reward our employees when they go out of their way to give not just *good* service but *superior* service to our guests. Help us decide who should be singled out for honors. All our employees wear name tags to assist you.

Name of employee_____

_____

Date of superior service_____

Time of superior service _____

Why service was superior _____

_____

_____

_____

_____

Name of guest _____

Room number _____

Signature _____

ing the customer's needs. The system has become more important than the reason for its existence — to serve the customer. A recent experience for us was in a restaurant that offered a full buffet lunch for $12.95 or soup and dessert from the buffet at $6.95. We informed the waitress we would be having the full buffet. However, following the soup, one of us chose to eliminate the main courses and have dessert. We told the waitress of this change when she came with our bill. Wrong! We received a thorough indoctrination on the functions of the computer wherein our original order resided and the complicated and time-consuming procedure it would take to retrieve and change it. We were thoroughly chastised but nevertheless reported her behavior to the manager. Most people in our place would have said nothing to the manager, never returned, but made a point to tell their friends.

Happily, some businesses are learning to be flexible. The business that can be flexible within the system will have greater success. For example, most people are not home during business hours. Companies that arrange home deliveries evenings or weekends offer a welcome service and a system that works for customers who cannot take a half day off work to wait for the delivery of the new washer. Banks and trust companies no longer keep "bankers' hours" from 10 a.m. to 3 p.m. The Canada Trust ad mentioned earlier points to their "friendly hours" by saying "We recognize your time pressures. .....savings, chequing, loan and mortgage business is done 8 to 8 Monday to Friday and 9 to 5 on Saturday... people hours, not bankers' hours."

e. CUSTOMERS DO NOT EXPECT TO BE EMBARRASSED

We were embarrassed when the receptionist told us to "sit" and when the waitress lectured us when we changed our order. Even though there was no real scene we felt childish and silly. We stated earlier that it costs more to regain a customer than to keep an existing one. Most customers are great people who do not set out to deliberately cause problems. The majority of complaints are legitimate and should be treated as such. Too often employees take problems or complaints personally and react defensively. If a situation means more work or a change of routine, as in the case of our problem with the waitress, they vent their frustration on the customer rather than biting their tongues and making the changes.

Complaints about products or performance often anger the service employees who react in a manner that embarrasses or angers the customer. A woman we know has been a very good client of a clothing boutique and had introduced many of her friends who in turn purchased several pricey items. However, when she was not satisfied with the way a garment had been shortened and hemmed, she returned it for correction and was told by the clerk that she was picky, demanding, and that the garment needed no correction. Angry and embarrassed she left the garment at the store. A letter of apology from the owner and an offer to replace the garment did not completely quell her anger. In the meantime, she has told all her friends about the incident. The boutique owner should seriously consider the clerk's employment, for over the past year the customer and her friends have spent an average of $600 per visit to the boutique.

f. CUSTOMERS DO NOT EXPECT TO BE TREATED WITH INDIFFERENCE, BIAS, OR PREJUDICE

Customers come in all shapes, sizes, ages, and colors. All have the right to expect similar service. You and your employees should consider the following:

(a) Children should have the same rights as all other customers. They should receive the same service no matter what the size of the purchase. How else will they grow up to be good, well-mannered, loyal customers? Take them in turn, treat them in a friendly manner, and take their purchases seriously.

(b) Most elderly people have all their faculties yet many service employees shout at them or talk as if they did not exist. Both our mothers are active eighty-six-year-olds. One visits Las Vegas at least twice a year, the other is so busy, her children have to make an appointment to see her. Nothing embarrasses them or us more than to have clerks or waitresses ask us what our mothers would like: "Would she like to see something in blue?" We reply, "Ask her. She's going to wear it and it's her money that will pay for it." Don't talk down to the elderly or patronize them. If they are on their own it is obvious that they are independent, bright, and active. If they are with someone, take your cue from them as to the older person's hearing and mobility.

(c) What we have said about children and the elderly also applies to the physically and mentally handicapped. Take your cue from the fact they are on their own, or from their care giver. You may have to take more time to listen carefully. Be sure to make eye contact with the person in the wheelchair. Do not shout at the blind. Shouting will not make them see. Be considerate, never condescending.

(d) Stereotyping customers whether because of their age or handicap is one concern. The other is the danger of stereotyping customers because of race. Owners, managers, and employees who have racial prejudices and biases can seriously jeopardize customer relations, even break the law. A very successful professional Asian woman who looks younger than she is has related to us some of her experiences with this problem, more prevalent than most of us realize. Carol (pseudonym) was born in Canada as were her parents. She is well regarded in her position as a tax lawyer and always dresses immaculately. Holidaying in a large city, she was shopping in an exclusive shoe store. When she lifted up a shoe to check the price sticker, a clerk flew across the store, took the shoe from her hand, and, shaking her finger, said in a loud voice, "No touchee!" Imagine, in 1990! Carol calmly turned and in her beautiful English replied, "I cannot comprehend what you are saying, but I can interpret your actions. As a lawyer, I remind you there are laws governing actions such as yours."

g. WHEN CUSTOMER EXPECTATIONS ARE UNREALISTIC

There are times when customers expect the impossible, which as the old adage goes, "takes a little longer." Some expectations cannot be fulfilled no matter how much time is taken. Unrealistic expectations may be a demand for a product or service that you do not produce or offer. The customer may want to "deal with the owner" who is located in another city or "will not talk to a woman." If you have only women employees you won't be able to meet their expectations. Customers may expect you to baby-sit while they shop, get their hair done, visit the doctor or dentist. That is not a usual service offered by clerks, hairstylists, or nurses. Kindly, but firmly advise your customers of the services you *do not give.*

    (a) Keep calm

    (b) Get the unrealistic customers away from the rest of your clients who may not realize the customer is making unrealistic demands. Unrealistic, demanding customers often like an audience.

    (c) Be empathetic

    (d) Offer alternative solutions

(e) Be firm but helpful

Cathy in the cartoon by Cathy Guisewite is the ultimate consumer. In one cartoon she makes unrealistic demands: "Do you have it in purple? Will you pull down all of them out of the boxes so I can see if they are exactly the same?" etc. The clerk has a store employee remove Cathy from the store, drive her home, lock her inside, and decorate her Christmas tree in return for the promise that she stay out of the store for 11 days. Upon her return home, Cathy announces that the selection at the store isn't that good but they are offering more customer service. Somehow, no matter how unrealistic the customer's expectations are, you have to be perceived as offering good customer service.

h. FULFILLED EXPECTATIONS FILL THE TILL

When you meet your customers' expectations they continue to buy from you and recommend your products and services to others. When you budget your business dollars budget less for advertising and more to keeping your customers by meeting their expectations through well-trained employees.

Consider the reasons for customer loss:

- 1% die
- 3% move
- 5% buy from a friend or relative
- 9% preferred another model
- 14% had a service problem that was not resolved
- 68% left because they felt employees were disinterested in giving service

These are statistics from the automotive industry but are applicable to other businesses as well. As you can see 68% left, not because of an unsolved problem, but because they were treated in the manner that did not meet their expectations. If those 68% had been turned into satisfied, loyal, repeat customers, the till would have rung up more sales, without spending advertising dollars. Solve the problems of the 14% and you've managed to retain all customer losses over which you have control.

CASE STUDY

John and Mary realized that surveying their customers in order to meet their expectations would be an ongoing process. Initially, they would discover what potential customers expect from a store like theirs. Later on, they could rate customer satisfaction, get customer opinion regarding products and services, and obtain ideas about new ones.

What they didn't realize at first was that their surveys would reveal a great deal about themselves and their employees, for people buy from people, not stores.

4

THE VALUE OF SERVICE

Of the 12.6 million new jobs created in the United States since 1982, 85% were in the service industry. The growth in the number of two-income families has resulted in mass consumer services in travel, eating, and entertainment. New technology like computers, including training and software, has created services that were unheard of 20 years ago.

The result of these two changes in our society — the two-income family and more service-oriented businesses — is multiplied demands for service. Two-income families want convenience and quick, personal service. When they don't get it, the result is friction between frontline people and customers.

In large centers, anonymity can provide protection for those who give bad service: telephones can be hung up; it is impossible to argue with a recorded message; the copy machine mechanic is never the same person twice in a row. In small towns where you have a limited number of customers, buyer and seller know they will be meeting each other again and again. Service has a name and a face, and, more important, it has a reputation.

As we move into the twenty-first century, large service companies in large centers are beginning to recognize that service has a value, a dollar value, which is a conclusion the small service company in the small town recognized years ago when it hoisted the sign over the store that read "The Customer Is Number One" and always treated its clientele accordingly.

Measuring the value of good customer service may seem an impossible task. If you have a product to sell that is needed by a certain buying public, then, in theory, all you have to do is let the public know (advertise), sell it to them, and that is that. But it is not as simple as that. As we said earlier, people buy more than things; they buy expectations. They expect that what they buy will give them the benefits the seller or manufacturer promised and that it will work as promised. They also expect that if the product does not perform or produce as promised, the seller or manufacturer will make good on that promise.

If you are selling the same product as your competitor, the difference in success will be measured by how the customer is treated, both during and after the sale. Initially, you and your competitor start evenly matched. But it is the intangible cosseting and concern, the customer service, that adds value and makes the buyer return again and again. Then you have a very measurable assessment of service: the bottom line — the repeat customer — money — greater profits.

a. SETTING A VALUE ON YOUR SERVICE

Customer service is not a straight line that begins when the customer sees or hears your advertisement and ends with the sale. It must continue long after the sale is made — until the next sale is made and then it must begin again.

Good customer service works in a circle, not a straight line. For example, suppose you are getting married and you seek out a photographer through an advertisement you have seen or on the recommendation of a friend. The photographer takes the pictures of your wedding. You like the pictures and buy those you want. For many photographers, that would be the end of the transaction. But a wise photographer, with a customer service program, will keep in touch with you, letting you know when the studio is offering special events and sales. The photographer knows that, in time, you will want new pictures taken. You may start a family and want baby pictures. From there, you might want to commemorate anniversaries, birthdays, and graduations. It goes on from there, through the lifetime of your family and your family members. Good service creates a ripple effect. One circle can start another circle of new customers.

In setting a value on your customer service, you must first recognize that customers are self-centered. They really do not care about your problems. They care about their own problems and they want them solved. Customer loyalty, which translates into return buyers, comes from providing the products that solve problems and from providing service that satisfies customer expectation at all times. A good service plan has the system, both physical and procedural, that employees can use to meet their customers' expectations.

b. SETTING A VALUE ON CUSTOMER CONTACT

A customer relations program must first place a value on each contact the customer has with your people. The fewer contacts the customer has with your employees, the greater must be the quality of each contact. When a customer is buying a dress in a store, for example, the clerk is usually the only person she has contact with. If the clerk is rude, uninterested, or not cooperative, the customer judges the whole store by that one contact. The more contacts the customer has with personnel, the greater the opportunity for breakdown in customer service or, conversely, for repair of damaged customer service.

For example, when you go to the movies, you buy your ticket from the ticket seller, you give your ticket to the usher, and you buy your popcorn from someone else. If the ticket seller is rude, you may forget it if you are treated with special care by the usher and the popcorn seller. On the other hand, if the usher is also rude, you may not be placated by a gracious popcorn seller, for you have already had two bad encounters.

Wise business leaders recognize this kind of situation as three opportunities for good customer relations and they emphasize the importance of service to every employee.

Every member of your organization must place a value on each opportunity they have to meet the customer or client. One dissatisfied customer will tell ten friends about the poor service or product. Those ten will tell ten more and soon your business reputation will snowball into an implacable negative value. Companies like Sony, IBM, General Electric, and Whirlpool long ago recognized service as a marketing tool — part of the product sale. They place a high value on the service component. Maytag uses service as a major part of their advertising — the product is so good it leaves the Maytag repairman with nothing to do — but still the company is selling a service.

c. SERVICE AS A PRODUCT

If you find it difficult to place a value on service, think of it as a product:

(a) Service is produced at the instant of delivery. You can't keep boxes of it on the shelf. Like electricity, you must produce it on demand.

(b) Service is delivered at the point of contact with the customer, by the frontline people, often beyond the control or influence of management or supervision.

(c) Service must be experienced by the customer at the moment it is delivered. It can't be sent out on approval.

(d) Service cannot be recalled, like a car for example. No one can bring it back for repairs. (You can offer apologies, but it's not the same. However, take heart; 95% of customers will buy again if a complaint is handled quickly and to their satisfaction.)

(e) Service is subjective. One person's idea of good service will differ from another's. You have to be prepared to deliver service to meet the varying standards: all sizes, all colors, in stock at all times!

d. THE VALUE OF EMPLOYEE PARTICIPATION

Remember that over 50% of customers rely on the opinions of their friends. Happy customers will be pleased to recommend you. The intangible service becomes tangible in the new customers you generate through your "product."

Barkers Fine Dry Cleaning in Calgary has a way of measuring the value of a unique customer service which they look upon as a product. They provide coupons for one free dry cleaning to exclusive boutiques to give to their customers who buy an item from those particular boutiques. The follow-through that gives this service value is most important. When the customer brings the garment into Barkers to be cleaned for free, the customer treatment is first class. If they return to have their other clothing cleaned, Barkers have created a new, satisfied customer.

When a beauty parlor tried a similar scheme, it backfired. Young sales people handed out coupons door to door that gave the purchaser cut rates on beauty services. But the beauty parlor had not convinced their employees of the benefits of the plan. The employees, who were paid a commission on their work, received less money from the coupon holders and they were not convinced that the coupons might bring in more business in the long run. When the coupon customers made their appointments, they were greeted with derision. In several instances when callers mentioned the coupons while trying to make appointments, they were told that there were no openings with any operator so the cards became valueless. Bad publicity kept customers away instead of creating new ones.

Selling the value of service to employees must be your first consideration. In order to give service a value, the employees must be part of evaluating procedure. When taxi owners and drivers did this kind of evaluation, they realized that they had a poor reputation for customer service, so they developed their "Miami Nice" customer relations training program for taxi drivers. The rewards of the program were so great that it became U.S.A. Nice and is now being used in Canada as well.

When you and your employees place a high value on service, the result is profit. In order to offer service that has value, you and your employees must consider service to be a product. That product is "sold" every time an employee has contact with a customer. Enthusiastic, cooperative personnel who know the value of service and who work together in harmony attract customers. Instead of having the company go to the market, the market comes to the company, and the company becomes more profitable.

e. EVALUATING YOUR SERVICE

You, your supervisors, and your managers need to ask the following questions and come to a consensus on the answers.

(a) How many employees do my clients or customers come in contact with before the sale is completed?

(b) How many employees do clients or customers come in contact with after the sale is completed? (Delivery, service, etc.)

(c) If one of those people stopped the sale from being completed, what minimum value, in dollars, could the company lose? (Your lowest product price.)

(d) If one of those people stopped the sale from happening, what maximum value, in dollars, could the company lose? (Your highest product price.)

(e) What would be the average loss of a sale? (Total of the minimum plus the maximum divided by two.)

(f) Based on the average loss of a sale, if the disgruntled customer told 10 other people (potential clients) what would be the total loss of the sale? (Multiply the average cost by 11: that is, the loss of the sale to the initial customer plus the potential loss of 10 customers.)

(g) Divide that total loss (answer to (f)) by the number of employees a customer contacts before, during, and after the sale. You now have the value of each customer contact. True, it is hypothetical, but it gives you an idea of the dollar value that good service can bring to your company.

CASE STUDY

When John and Mary evaluated the service at the ABC Shoppe, they found that the customer usually came into contact with just one employee, right at the point of sale, with no follow-up contact for delivery or service. The lowest priced item in their store was a pair of small scissors that could be carried in a pocket or purse ($5.95). The highest priced item was a silk blouse ($398.00). Therefore, the average loss of sale would be $201.98. The total loss of one dissatisfied customer could mean a potential loss of $2,221.78 ($201.98 x 11 lost customers). Seen in those terms, John and Mary realized the value of good customer service; it meant the difference between paying the rent or not!

5
MANAGING THE PROCESS

A major precept of customer relations is to make sure you provide what the customer really wants and needs, and to do it before your competition does. It's a way of adding longevity to your business, a way of surviving. Anyone who wants to remain in business practices customer relations — keeping customers satisfied by organizing, presenting, and delivering a product or service for their benefit. It's simple, it's common sense, and it works.

a. COMBINING HIGH TECH AND HIGH TOUCH

Businesses stay in business by combining two techniques — the mechanical and the humanistic. Or, if you like, the high tech and the high touch.

1. Crunching numbers

On the high tech side is the continual monitoring of market conditions and comparisons of location, availability, price, competition, and all the other items in the business mix in the particular geographic market. Much of what is done in this area is paper-based or computer-oriented.

You need this solid background information to know how you're doing compared to the competition. It's also valuable to have this data so that you can measure improvements in your public image or service quality in economic terms (i.e., at the cash register). You have to be able to compare oranges with oranges.

While you're making these comparisons and while the improvements or adjustments are taking place, you have to keep a weather eye cocked to the task of enlarging your present customer base. But you have to manage the mechanical side of your business in such a way that you don't alienate your bread-and-butter clientele as the cost of gaining new business.

2. Dealing with people

The second technique is developing the "people" side of the business. This is the humanistic or high touch area, which includes all aspects of customer contact plus the hiring, firing, motivating, and training of your staff. It can also include one-on-one coaching and encouragement and replenishment of staff vitality and enthusiasm.

This interactive side of the business requires attention to intangible people values, rather than purely technical details. The high touch side of a business calls for different management skills — "people" skills. These are essential for good managers.

Add the high tech and high touch managing skills described above to the demands of planning, promotion, advertising, and ordering and you'll see why people look askance at the deceptively simple title of manager. There are as many definitions of a manager as there are managers. There is an equally large number of definitions of essential management skills for customer relations and almost as many books on the subject.

3. Managing the mix

As a manager, your prime customer relations requisite is to decide on and develop a program that will work for you. As each business is unique, so are the requirements for making that specific business successful.

So let's examine what we mean by managing for customer relations success and start with a couple of questions. Do you need all or any of the usually accepted management skills or the skills mentioned above? And, if so, which techniques will work best for you in your particular situation?

Some answers come easily because feedback is immediate. For example, when you're present at the scene (on the job), there is a personal sense of being in control — whether justified or not. You can feel that because you are at the center of the action, often personally directing traffic, you are managing the event.

Assuming this to be true, what happens when you are not there to stick-handle? How can you be sure your carefully crafted plans for service excellence are being followed? Is everybody doing what they are supposed to do? Are they working as a team ? Is everything running smoothly?

The real question is whether you can "manage" indirectly. Have you trained your staff and yourself well enough for you to be able to step away from your business? Do you have full confidence in your staff's ability to handle customers, and do it with the same care and concern you show yourself?

Perhaps the most significant question when delegating responsibilities is — will you get feedback if things aren't running smoothly? We pose this question because there's a pretty good chance you won't hear about it from your customer. Remember, 97% of unhappy customers just go away and don't return. And there's an equally good chance your staff may be reluctant to tell you if they bungled a transaction with a valued customer. So, a major management responsibility is to make sure you get feedback about how the business is going, even in your absence.

Let's assume you have confidence in your people to handle things well in their public contacts. Do they have enough confidence in your system that the concepts and values will be upheld, regardless of which individual represents the company at that particular moment?

What all these questions point out is the need for a definite focus on managing "in absentia" as well as managing "in person." It's the first category that causes most anxiety for managers. Yet it needn't be so, particularly if managers and service-givers can make the time to exchange a thought or two that will benefit both.

Managers need to acknowledge that solutions to problems that plague their business or their industry can often be found by those working closest to the source. The history of business and industry is full of tales of opportunities lost because managers either forgot or ignored, the vast pool of knowledge and skill just outside their office doors.

Conversely, there are also some exciting and dramatic stories of how organizations have turned their fortunes around by simply listening — listening to experienced people who had a solution and were waiting for someone with the sense to ask them. In other words, those facing a problem, those deeply involved in it, generally know the cause. More important, they frequently know the solution.

Obviously, then, it makes good sense to ask for their help. If you already have a customer relations program in place and you are really listening to your employees, good. If not, why not start today? Once the staff have overcome their initial skepticism, you'll find them eager to help.

If you're in the early stages of building a customer relations program, why not ask your people for help in the formative stages, during the planning and organizing phases? Get the benefit of their advice. It's the kind of advice for which many organizations pay huge consulting fees, but it could be available to you just for the asking.

Perhaps the biggest obstacle everyone faces is management ego. A manager should know all the answers, right? After all, that's what the title means, doesn't it — to come up with solutions? And anyhow, what do the people at the front counter know, they're not paid to think! It would be nice in our technologically advanced business world to think we had eliminated myopic management, but it is still with us and still surfaces. And when it does, everyone suffers — customer, employee, manager, director, and shareholder.

So, if your organization is one of the lucky ones whose business "vision" is improving and undergoing change and if you're willing to recognize the reservoir of skills and talents that's available at your finger tips, here's just one more rule — a rule that's so important it should be engraved on every manager's forehead: *when you've asked for help, sit back, shut up, and listen*. Listen carefully ... listen profitably. Listening is vital and feedback from employees essential if you wish to improve performance in satisfying customer needs.

The other critical element in managing customer relations is figuring out how to become a better manager in an area that is unfamiliar. Some companies offer their employees a CARE package, a collection of four commonly used words that are the basis of any good management program. The words are commitment, awareness, recognition, and evaluation. It's an acronym that will keep all staff members involved and interested.

b. COMMITMENT

Let's look at the first letter of our CARE package — commitment.

It's sad, but true, that many managers expect staff to be committed to every whim and idea emanating from the executive office. Unfortunately, just saying something doesn't make it so, as many companies have discovered to their chagrin.

Commitment and loyalty cannot simply be demanded, regardless of whether a product, idea, or action deserves support. Commitment isn't something you can buy or have installed. It is an attitude and a spirit that has to be earned and developed.

Often overlooked in discussions of customer relations is the role managers and leaders play in developing employee attitudes toward commitment. Leaders of any organization must set the tone — they must be shining examples. If they expect a commitment from others, not only must they voice their wholehearted support, but they must demonstrate it, too. If commitment to customer relations is to have any long-term relevance, managers need to eat it, breathe it, think it, and live it. Employees need to "see" concrete evidence of management's commitment both in word and deed.

There must be a clear perception that company commitment is 100%, from the top down. Without wholehearted commitment from management, it will be impossible to generate respect for the program or drum up the support needed to maintain it successfully once it has been launched.

You may be asking what degree of commitment we are talking about. Just how much commitment is needed to make a program work? A customer relations program must become a way of life, an inseparable, ingrained way of doing business. A customer relations program must evolve into a living policy and philosophy, refreshed, reviewed, renewed, and reinforced constantly by the leaders of the organization.

Let's assume that management commitment is alive, well, and in place at your company, having been proclaimed in word and deed. How, then, do you encourage commitment from other employees?

Get them involved. Ideally, get employees involved in the initial stages of planning, in the surveying, questioning, and analysis of the customer base. But failing that, it is vital, indeed it is crucial, to get them involved in the process of suggesting or making changes and improvements to the system. This way, not only will they add the wisdom of their experience, but they will be able to view the process in a proprietary way — as *their* changes to *their* system. When you can persuade employees to think in terms of "ours," and not "the company's," you've gone a long way toward establishing a solid customer relations foundation.

Managers must recognize that the most sensitive element in a customer relations system is that critical moment when the frontline employee goes eyeball to eyeball with the customer. That's decision time for both — the moment of truth — the fragile juncture when customer loyalty is on the line and can certainly be swayed by employee commitment.

Multiply that moment by the days, weeks, and months and you'll quickly appreciate the positive impact well-trained representatives have, especially those with the right attitude.

Now, take just a moment to consider Emma Employee.

Here's a person representing your organization, whether on the road, on the line, or behind a counter. And, at any given moment in the business day, for all intents and purposes, she *is* the organization, she *is* your company.

Picture her facing a barrage of flak, holding back anger and personal emotions, trying to think on her feet, trying to resolve a problem or develop a satisfactory solution to a customer complaint. Imagine her mentally measuring her answers against a written policy she may have read three or four years previously and hasn't seen since. While this is going on, an irate, vociferous customer is berating her.

As a manager responsible for customer relations, would you wish this, either for your customer or your employee? Would you relish being caught ill-prepared in a similar situation?

The obvious question arises, Would training help? Would empowerment help, a sharing of responsibility? Do you think it would it help you if you were faced with a similar situation?

The answer is an equally obvious yes!

As managers, we can answer all of the questions this chapter has posed and at the same time alleviate a large proportion of our customer relations problems with a two-fold commitment: commitment from management for timely, relevant, quality training, and commitment from employees to develop a personal awareness of the organization and their specific role in it.

Without commitment from both groups the best-laid plan will falter and eventually grind to a standstill.

c. AWARENESS

The simple solution to managing well is awareness. You have to be attuned to the total climate that surrounds your business — the people, the product, the competition, and the market.

Awareness means keeping track of what the competition is up to — what they are doing now and what they are proposing to do.

Awareness also means remaining conscious of and responsive to the impact of customer expectations on your business. You need to know not only what your customers need both individually and collectively, but also what they think about your product and your service.

Awareness means keeping abreast of employee expectations. What do they need in order to be your ambassadors? And what do they think about your organization ... its products, policies, and people? Just one of these areas is enough to keep managers on their toes; but together they are a real challenge.

Of the three, awareness of customer expectations demands priority. Ironically, organizations create high customer expectations with their own promotion efforts. When the promotion is successful, then they have to live up to the promises made — or implied. Once the expectation has been created, woe betide the organization that fails to deliver.

It is the mismanagement of customer expectations that leads to customer frustration and, ultimately, customer desertion, and mismanagement can occur anywhere in the organization, from the first phone call to the final delivery. Anyone can fumble the ball, of course, but smart business people discover how to recover, and then practice hanging on to the ball in the most difficult situations. And what a comforting thought to know that there are others on your team willing to help out.

And quite simply, that is the essence of good customer relations: It is a team effort. The whole organization must be aware that customer service is everybody's business — not just those on the front line, but all the people behind the scenes, too.

Every individual must realize that the quality of customer relations is quickly becoming a major factor in business decisions. Expectations will continue to climb as customers display a greater degree of sophistication. This means an organization's entire culture must emphasize the value of customer relations, and the fact that it can indeed mean the difference between survival and extinction.

Two brief incidents at the Riverside Hilton in New Orleans dramatically illustrate the value of personal warmth and sincerity in showing customers you care. Picture a gleaming lobby, a cooling breeze wafting through, and a weary seminar leader looking for a bite to eat. It's 7:30 p.m. and after a day on my feet I'm headed for the downstairs coffee shop. On the way down the escalator a lady from housekeeping is coming up the other side, dusting around the handrail.

As we approach each other she stops her dusting, gives me the biggest, warmest smile I've received in a decade, and says, "Now y'all have yourself a real nice evening."

As I thank her, I ask if the coffee shop is open and if they serve light snacks. She says, "They sure do. And they'll fix you the nicest, tastiest meal you've had in a long time." And again, I get the beaming smile.

What impresses me is the sincerity in the voice. I feel she is genuinely interested in helping me enjoy my evening. I'm not an interruption to her day, far from it. In fact, I am part of the reason she is there, part of the reason why she has a job, and I get the impression she is thanking me personally for the favor.

Well, I know I am going to have a "real nice" evening, and that I will enjoy the coffee shop. Events prove her right.

When I ask the waiter for something light he says, "I've got just the thing for you. The lasagna is great. You'll really enjoy it. I guarantee it."

What can I say? I've been softened up, and then sold. But what a pleasant way to be sold. I am a willing participant. I had been conditioned on the escalator and my expectations are fulfilled.

Now comes the finishing touch. As the waiter reverently places the plate in front of me, he says in a voice tinged with awe, "Doesn't that look wonderful?"

Then his enthusiasm bursts forth as he says, " I just know you're going to love it." What can I do? I do as I am told and I love it. It is wonderful.

The moral is that both individuals were aware their function was to make me feel good about being in their hotel, and from my point of view they were acting as though they were the owners.

They recognized that most people sag at the end of the day, particularly if they are from out of state and on a different time schedule. They lifted my spirits the best way they knew how — with the human voice, a warm human voice that said very clearly somebody cared.

The upshot was I spent the entire next morning interviewing managers at all levels quizzing them about the systems they used to keep employees effervescent and motivated. It hardly came as a surprise when I received the same courteous and considerate attention from each and every manager, despite some heavy pressures on them to meet deadlines.

I discovered that the Hilton's training program is exhaustive. It is detailed and time consuming. There are daily updates, weekly meetings, managers' meetings, staff meetings, and one-on-one briefings. Staff are encouraged to speak out, and the whole process hinges on two-way communication to solve problems, to inform each other, and to motivate by putting values into action. This is a considerable investment in human resources and in money. But if my experience is typical, others too will return.

If there's one simple rule for managers to follow to encourage awareness and enhance performance, it is this: Treat your employees the way you want them to treat your customers.

Like the folks at the Riverside Hilton, when employees feel good about their company they cannot help but show it. The lesson I learned is that the right tone of voice could have me eating lasagna every day.

d. RECOGNITION

This leads naturally into the third segment of our CARE package: R for recognition — one of the most powerful motivators available.

As individuals, we all seek recognition. Whether we are customers, clerks, owners, operators, investors, wives, husbands, or children, we want to be noticed and acknowledged. The need for recognition is a driving force in our lives.

It's no accident that the people who help us satisfy our needs are handsomely rewarded. We are drawn toward them and come to depend on them. As a manager, your function is to capitalize on the power of recognition and devise ways to make it work for you. Successful managers harmonize the policies, products, and services of their organizations and the skills and knowledge of their staffs with the needs of their customers. No small task, but attainable.

The music that will help encourage a "symphony" in your organization is the melody of timely recognition. And the best part is it doesn't have to be elaborate or expensive — just appropriate and sincere.

In companies of all sizes, an occasional "Thank you" often works wonders. A simple compliment in front of other staff members, or tickets to a show, or perhaps a complimentary dinner outing for excellent performance — these are inexpensive but valuable ways of building self-esteem and pride.

Acknowledging to customers that members of your staff are experts in their field and publicly voicing genuine praise can also work wonders when developing a commitment to the team concept.

Recognition must be an essential building block in any customer relations program, regardless of the organization's size.

e. EVALUATION

The fourth management element in our CARE package is evaluation: identifying what works and what doesn't, and devising methods of measuring the success of programs and the effectiveness of employees. Assessment and measurement are important because they let us see if we are satisfying the objectives of our customer relations plan or even moving toward our goals. It is also important to realize that measurement programs or evaluation scales can be deceptive in that they can be innocently designed to reflect customer satisfaction exclusively.

While there's no argument happy customers are your prime goal, don't concentrate solely on the public's impression of the company to the exclusion of other important information. You need to know more than just that. You need to know how well you did as an employer or employee, how you came across as a member of the team, and how well your business came across as an organization. With this knowledge, you can continue to improve.

Again, build on the basis of getting all employees involved. It's been shown that methods for measuring the performance of people are more equitable and usually more relevant when the people being evaluated have a hand in developing and designing the criteria. The Swedish car manufacturer, Volvo, has proven this repeatedly with its small work groups for assembling automobiles. In filling vacancies or replacing a member of the assembly group, new prospects are evaluated by the present members of the group who have the ultimate decision on who will join them.

This group referendum process gives a boost to the self-worth of the successful candidate, but at the same time imposes a moral and professional obligation. It's an unwritten contract for personal responsibility and commitment to the people who have voted their faith in your ability to live up to pre-determined standards. If you let things slide, you let the team down.

f. SUMMARY

In summary, employees will be a valuable source of both knowledge and ideas on enhancing your customer relations.

If asked, they will be equally responsible in proposing ways to measure the value of programs and in devising methods to measure the effectiveness of people involved in the program.

It simply boils down to this. You are planning and discussing not only their present jobs, but their future, and if they can influence and improve that process in any way, then they will support it. By inference, the way to get commitment is to ask for input.

When you ask for help, you've taken the first heady step toward getting commitment. How can anybody not support a good idea that affects them in a positive manner — particularly if it's an idea of their own?

Commitment, awareness, recognition, and evaluation make a CARE package that speaks for itself. It also speaks for you, in that you've made a very positive statement about your management capabilities and you've recognized that customer relations, like any business segment, must be managed, and managed well, to be successful.

CASE STUDY

Both John and Mary soon realized that to build a sound business that would encourage growth and develop customer loyalty, their entire staff must be involved and committed to managing customers' "total experience" at the ABC Shoppe.

This meant viewing the experience through customers' eyes.

Unsure of how to proceed, they set aside one Sunday and brainstormed a plan. They decided that both owners, John and Mary, should visit businesses similar to theirs to evaluate the shopping environment of their competitors. They drew up a list of stores they might visit, then whittled this down to a list of stores with similar floor space, traffic, location, and clientele. To ensure they weren't focussing on too narrow a segment of business, they included a couple of larger stores with well-established customer bases and three smaller outlets that enjoyed good reputations. They also gathered consumer comments from ABC's friends and clients.

To develop a level of consistency in evaluating the service their competitors were offering, they worked out a simple checklist that covered appearance of the store (inside and out), appearance of the staff, layout of merchandise, friendliness and helpfulness of staff (attitude), knowledge of product, and willingness to accommodate unusual requests to help the customer.

The results of those visits, along with copies of current advertising and information about successful promotions developed by their competitors gave the ABC owners a benchmark for evaluating and comparing their own store and ideas for improving its performance.

In a burst of inspiration, John had also suggested having family or friends visit the ABC Shoppe and assess the performance of store staff using the same evaluation scoresheet as John and Mary were using to evaluate competitors.

The idea was good, but when it was announced to the staff — after the fact — it met with a decidedly cool reception. The staff were surprised and then annoyed. Some said it left the impression they "weren't to be trusted."

John moved quickly to mend fences. He admitted they hadn't thought to include staff in planning or to tell them about the store visits. Nor had they given any thought to the possibility that the staff might feel they'd been put under a microscope.

Fears were calmed by frank and open discussion of the reasons for the survey. John and Mary admitted that in retrospect it made sense to include staff in the planning and apologized for the omission. They pointed out that they were under the microscope too, as they didn't know the identity of some of their survey visitors, but admitted they had had an advantage because they knew evaluators would show up at some time.

Later, when the group reviewed the survey answers and ratings, they were pleased to find themselves in the top one-third category for providing customer satisfaction. More important, the staff now had examples of management techniques that really worked and knew the changes to be made if ABC was to manage a customer's total shopping experience successfully.

6

DEVELOPING A PROFITABLE CUSTOMER RELATIONS PROGRAM

Any plan for improvement needs people. You can lavish care on trend lines, graphs, pie charts, and diagrams and lovingly produce blueprints that are works of art, but, eventually, somebody, somewhere, somehow has to transform those good intentions into reality. That is when you must depend on your employees.

It takes human energy and ingenuity to turn the potential into practice, to make the promise come alive, to lift fragile words off paper and turn them into a dynamic human force. Woe betide the company that thinks the hard part is over when the plans are approved. The task has just begun.

Many companies, enamored of their plans, pay homage to the piles of paper, while ignoring the human aspect of the process. They just assume people will understand. Even more perilous is the assumption that people will automatically agree with the proposals. The result is their energetic program evolves into a static display in the basement vault, and once in a while the senior people must muse on what might have been if only the "others" had cooperated.

So let's put the horse back in front of the cart and start with your most important resource: your people.

a. DEVELOPING EMPLOYEE SUPPORT

1. Getting their attention

Wise organizations know cooperation is the keystone for progress. They realize and acknowledge that their employees are the vehicle by which the organization can prosper and grow. But to do so, the employees must also prosper and grow, so it makes sense for management to invest in the development of its people by enlarging their knowledge base and including them in the planning process.

It's a two-way street. As employees' confidence and skills improve so do their contributions to the company because they have a keener interest in their careers. The more they feel they are contributing the more they feel a part of the total company family; they are investing a portion of themselves in the organization.

Have you ever heard a person proudly talk about "my company"? There is the often-told story of Marshall Field, owner of the giant Field's Department store chain in Chicago, who was walking through the various departments of the store and overheard an employee's little girl talking to another about "my daddy's" store and "my daddy's" customers. The child's mother recognized Mr. Field and started to apologize for her daughter's chatter about the store belonging to her daddy. Mr. Field interrupted her by saying, "If only I could get more employees to think of the store as their own."

Despite what most pessimists say, the proprietary glow still burns in the hearts of many employees. It's a precious resource, and you can rekindle that flame, then fan it into a bright and glowing attitude, by letting employees know they are important.

But first you need to get their attention. Old-style management would have suggested that a two-by-four across the back of the neck was a good way to get attention. Maybe it would work for a while, but the attention would be fleeting, at most, and soon pushed out of mind by resentment of the crude way it was handled.

Today we have more effective ways to get people's attention. In 1979, Studs Terkel, author of the best-selling book

Working, spoke in San Francisco at the annual convention of the International Association of Business Communicators. He talked about how he had interviewed workers all across the United States. In one instance he ate lunch with a steelworker, perched high on the steel framework of a burgeoning new skyscraper. When questioned about the major component missing from his job, the steelworker said it was recognition. "When the building is completed," he said, "nobody will ever know I worked on it. I can't even bring my children to show them my handiwork because it will be all encased in concrete."

Questioned further, the steelworker came up with an idea to counter the lack of recognition. He suggested that a stainless steel strip with the name of every contributor engraved on it be fastened to the side of the building where it could be easily seen.

When you think about it, we're not talking about business logic, but emotion, one of the most powerful forces we can harness. People make decisions based on emotion, then justify them afterward with logic. First you need to win your employees' hearts, then you'll be able to capture their minds.

So, to firmly grasp the interest of your people and then maintain it, you need to give them recognition. You need a steel strip firmly fixed in everybody's mind that tells them over and again that they are important and they are recognized.

2. Getting them motivated

It has been said that you cannot motivate other people...they have to motivate themselves.

This may be so, but you can certainly provide the ammunition for your employees or co-workers to motivate themselves. It is part of a manager's role to show people how to get excited, enthused, and energetic about their new and expanded responsibilities; and we do mean show them, not tell them. Yet few managers know where to begin.

The pivotal word is belonging. A sense of belonging is crucial as a motivating factor. When people feel they are contributing their personal talents to a worthwhile endeavor, then they have a stake in that enterprise. They adopt a personal responsibility, become committed, and, best of all, start developing pride — pride in themselves and pride in the work they perform. To get people motivated, you have to put them back in the picture, convince them that their contribution is valuable, give them responsibility, and allow them to use their creativity.

In the past, creativity and thinking by employees was viewed almost as subversive. How many times have you heard a manager or employer say, "Why would they want to think anyway? We do it for them. They just have to show up and do what they're told."

Yet employees do need to do much more than that. They need to reason and make subjective judgment calls and decisions that require emotional considerations. As managers finally acknowledge this, the feudal attitude in business and industry is yielding to a growing awareness that the real resource of any organization is its people. They are no longer pawns but important centers of influence. Properly motivated they can be the difference between success or failure, between profit or loss.

3. Getting them involved

Get your employees involved at the outset in helping to define and then develop your plan. Ask them for ideas. Have them on the task force or the steering committee, whatever you call it, but get them involved.

Most people would agree that commitment is paramount to any sustained program of customer relations, but commitment is not achieved on a casual basis. There has to be a reason for people to commit themselves to an ideal or a cause. They can't commit themselves wholeheartedly unless they know what it is they are committing themselves to and why. In other words, they must understand the reason why you are asking for their assistance.

If they can develop an understanding of the plan and their role in it, involvement can be the next step. Get them involved in the early stages of planning.

Here's a note of warning. People will only be as effective as the leaders they follow. They will not commit themselves further or involve themselves more deeply than their immediate managers do. So if you have managers who are only paying lip service to newly developed plans, lip service will be the order of the day for all their subordinates.

4.   Getting them encouraged

Encouragement is another powerful business tool, and yet, sadly, it's the one most overlooked. It's not neglected deliberately; in fact, most people recognize what a potent force it can be, but it is easy to say, "Well, we don't have the time or the inclination right now. Besides, next year looks much brighter...with more potential."

Let's state it frankly. Without encouragement, people become robots, performing acceptable tasks at barely acceptable levels. Why? They have no interest invested in their work, and by implication the organization has no interest invested in them. Yet time and again we hear managers complain that loyalty seems to have evaporated along with the ethic of "an hour's pay for an hour's work."

Ask yourself if loyalty has really gone the way of the dodo bird and silently slipped away, or has it been stifled, crushed, and ignored in the blind pursuit of profit and the rush for clinical efficiency? In a solid-state world we sometimes forget we're dealing with fluid-state people.

Academic theories aside, if loyalty has disappeared or died, can it be restored or revitalized? It has been done before, but it has taken time, and, above all, commitment — long-term commitment. Why not avoid the pain of restoration? Start off on the right foot. Begin with encouragement — given sincerely and at appropriate times.

b. PUTTING IT TOGETHER

We've talked about the steps necessary to get employees interested in a customer service plan. They include getting the employees' attention, getting them motivated, getting them involved, and then getting them encouraged. The question is how to tie all this together so it makes sense and makes them want to be a part of the program.

Tell them what's in it for them! Talk about benefits, the rewards, the prestige they will gain by becoming active in this program. As you talk about the benefits, emphasize the personal aspects of involvement, how they can personally grow by playing an active role as an individual or on the team, and about becoming committed.

Then, to ensure they remain committed once they are involved in the planning process, help them view the customer relations program as theirs. If they can recognize themselves or their contribution in some aspect of the plan, then it will become "their" plan. Design a recognition program by considering how employees will be rewarded for —

(a) providing input to the formulation of the program (i.e., serving on a planning committee or task force),

(b) implementing the program,

(c) maintaining the program (you will want to review this after three months, six months, and one year),

(d) increasing revenue through the customer relations program,

(e) creating a stronger public image (e.g., involvement in the community outside of business that reflects positively on the business), and

(f) augmenting the program with new ideas, new methods, new procedures. ("Suggestion box" contributions that are used should be rewarded. Continued committee work for monitoring and assessment should be rewarded.)

Recognition can be provided by verbal praise, monetary gifts, plaques, etc. Rewards should be given before peers to fully recognize the contribution of the employee and to provide an incentive for other employees.

You may decide that an annual meeting is the most appropriate place for public recognition of major achievements. Alternatively, you may decide on a less formal semi-annual meeting in addition to the larger meeting to increase the interest at the local level. Stories and feature articles in the organization's newsletter are an ideal and economical way to show appreciation. Small dinner parties and special events are also good ways to focus attention on your commitment to the program.

We said earlier that good communication is a journey, not a destination. The same applies to encouragement and the benefit is that it pays off — big.

When you include your people from the outset, the bonus is you will receive advice from the frontline troops, the people in the trenches who look eyeball to eyeball with your customers on a daily basis. They are the experts. Why not tap that knowledge? It's a compliment to your employees that you want to listen to them and their advice.

But it's also a big boost to their self-esteem when you acknowledge their expertise by including their suggestions in your customer service plan. When a person's self-esteem rises, so does the morale in that particular office or area. It rubs off on others because as humans we don't want to be left out...we don't want to miss anything.

c. A SIMPLE PLAN THAT WORKS

Most simple plans work. It is when we get fancy and add frills, or when we plan to impress, rather than express, that we run into trouble. So, assuming you have your employees onside, that they want to become involved, and that they are anxious to get rolling, then here is a simple formula that works. You can add to it, enlarge it, reduce it, change it, or adapt it, depending on what you and your people decide; but it will help you get started, and you can start right away.

Most problem solving starts with research; we have chosen the RACE formula to help you get yourself launched. RACE stands for Research, Action, Communication, and Evaluation.

To follow the formula, you need to work through a series of steps.

1. Know intimately the policies, goals, and objectives of your organization.

2. Analyze your various customers, clients, and employees and their significance to you.

3. Assess your reputation with each of your customers, clients, employees, and the potential for improvement.

4. Decide what actions are required and the strategy to achieve them.

5. Plan your program.

6. Implement the program.

7. Monitor its progress and results.

8. Revise and adjust where necessary.

If you follow through on the eight steps above, you will find out why people respond to you and your business in a particular manner and how you can design your responses to get them on your side rather than in opposition.

Let's go through each of the eight areas in more detail.

1. Know the policies, goals, and objectives of your organization

It may sound redundant to say you need to know your organization, but ask 20 employees coming out of an office at 5:30 p.m. why they are in business and you might be surprised at the replies. If you know your organization thoroughly, you can plan for its growth. You can talk about it sensibly and confidently and with conviction. And, frankly, you better know more about your business than your competitors because they will be exploiting your weaknesses before you know that those weaknesses exist. Above all, don't forget to communicate your thoughts and ideas. (See chapter 9.)

2. Analyze your customers, clients, and employees

Once you have a solid grasp on who you are, what you do, and why, then you can turn your attention to knowing your customers, clients, and employees. Examine their wants and needs, their likes and dislikes, their incomes, attitudes preferences, or biases. The more you know about them, the more your plans can reflect their lifestyles. You can analyze them, examine the problems, differences, and barriers between them and you, and then determine the potential for improvement. And let's face it, is there a single organization in North America that couldn't stand having its image polished? Remember to communicate your findings.

3. Assess your reputation

See if you can discover the reason for your reputation, good or bad. Is it justified, can it be changed, are there any benefits if it is changed? What is your image now? What would you like it to be? What do people really think of your organization? Communicate your results or findings.

4. Decide what actions are required and the strategy needed

What can you do to improve your image? How can you develop your potential? Communicate your strategy to employees.

5. Plan your program

Use input and advice from all employees to develop a customer service program. Your aim should be to get both employees and customers thinking in terms of "my business." Remember, communicate your plans.

6. Implement the program

The implementation of your plan should receive the same care and attention as the planning process. How and when you put the plan into effect can affect the overall success of your venture. It has to be done logically, deliberately, step by step, anchoring one segment firmly in place before moving on to the next. If there are delays, tell people and tell them why. If changes are needed, keep them informed. Better still, ask for help. Continually communicate the process.

7. Monitor its progress

Monitoring a customer service program requires fortitude. It requires "stick-to-it-ness," persistence, a hang-in-there attitude to overcome the tendency to settle back in your chair. When so much energy has been poured into the previous steps of planning the process, the urge is to launch it and leave it...if the darn thing floats then you have been successful. Unfortunately, this is the point where many finely crafted programs founder; much the same as launching a luxury liner: initially it's the keel that slides down, with much work still to be done inside and up top. When you launch your program you will find much work still to be done: fine-tuning, polishing, and plugging leaks. And as with a ship, maintenance is ongoing. Communicate progress.

8. Revise and adjust

Revising a plan can be difficult, but if it needs to be done, then do it quickly. Once again, get input and solutions from your employees. You don't do anyone a favor by waffling when you should be deciding. If changes are necessary, act promptly. Let employees know about the changes and the reasons they were adopted. When you keep people informed, they are more sympathetic to the cause and to the frustration you encounter. Often they will be moved enough to put forward alternative suggestions, particularly if they view their actions as one team member coming to the aid of another. Again, communicate changes, and the reasons for them.

d. DO-IT-YOURSELF FLOWCHART

The figure on page 77 is a flowchart to help you get your plan started. Pick the topics and areas you feel most appropriate to your situation, but do it now. Roughly chart out your ideas, and then read on for ideas on setting goals and implementing your ideas.

CASE STUDY

John and Mary decided it was time to involve the employees of the ABC Shoppe. A meeting seemed a good way to start to review the store's performance and listen to employees' concerns too. To help understand the store's objectives, John prepared some simple charts.

They held a staff meeting at a time that was agreeable to all. The staff was paid for attending the meeting. John reviewed the six months they had been in business and he pointed out that while revenues were constant, they signified no growth and it was obvious that there was a lack of customer return and loyalty.

Mary reported the results on their evaluation of service (see chapter 4), and John introduced the idea of a customer service program and how to go about preparing one for the store. Using a flowchart he designed himself, John discussed each step. Both he and Mary encouraged all the staff to take part in the discussion.

While everybody agreed there was a need for improved customer relations, it was immediately apparent there was also a need to set some goals for the program. They did that by following the advice in the next chapter.

FIGURE #1
DO-IT-YOURSELF FLOWCHART

START BY RESEARCHING THESE AREAS

Business organization
Management objectives and organization
Suppliers and creditors
Business policies
The products or services we supply
Community
Employees (and labor unions)
Stockholders
Customer/client relations
Competitors
Marketing program
Customers

↓

THEN ANALYZE WHAT YOU HAVE DISCOVERED IN TERMS OF

Business objectives
Customer service problems and interests
Capabilities — the company's, the staff's
Growth factors

↓

**WHEN YOU KNOW YOUR STRENGTHS AND WEAKNESSES,
THEN DESIGN YOUR STRATEGY TO ACHIEVE**

Business objectives
Marketing objectives

↓

PLAN THE PROGRAM TO GET RESULTS

Objectives
Customers/clients to be reached
Implementing the program
Methods to be used
Results expected

↓

IMPLEMENT THE PLAN

People
Place
Time

↓

MONITOR AND ADJUST

Check
Review
Revise

7
SETTING GOALS FOR YOUR BUSINESS

Most business people will say frankly that they are in business to make money, and there is nothing wrong with that. But the manner in which you make that money can be affected by the image and reputation the company wishes to create. If you are in business to make money in a very short time, image and reputation may not be a high priority. But if you plan to be around for any length of time, then they become very important. Before you can have a successful customer relations program, you must make some very important decisions about image and reputation, quality and performance. The Japanese have shown us that putting quality first did not increase costs, but actually increased profits. The Disney corporation sets very high standards for the image, reputation, and quality of its operations of Disneyland and Disney World. The result has been world-wide esteem and a very healthy business.

a. WHY ARE YOU IN BUSINESS?

Answer these questions, honestly. No one is looking over your shoulder.

   (a) Am I in business to make a profit?

   (b) Am I in business for the long haul?

   (c) Is my personal reputation important to me?

   (d) Is my company's reputation important to me?

   (e) Is customer satisfaction important to the success of my business?

(f) Is the repeat customer important to my business?

(g) Do I plan to be in this particular town or city for a period of time?

(h) If my business expanded, would my reputation and my company's reputation in this area still be important to me?

John and Mary of our case study answered all these questions with a strong yes. If *you* answered yes to the above questions, then image and reputation are important to you and your business. But you need to define clearly what you want that image and reputation to be. This should be the first step in the research for your customer service program. Ask yourself the following questions, then have your employees answer the same questions, individually.

(a) Describe what this business is in business for.

(b) Why would you recommend people do business with this organization?

(c) Why do you work for this company?

(d) What is the greatest satisfaction you get from working for this company?

Compare your responses to those of your employees. Is there a correlation of perception or a marked difference? Employees who have a genuine interest and pride in their work and the company project that pride, and it is this same pride that builds a company's positive reputation.

CASE STUDY

When John and Mary compared their answers to those of their employees, they found some differences. While June's answers were more like their own and showed a strong leaning toward the customer, recognition of good service, and the satisfaction of doing a job well, Jim's perception was solely to make money for himself and the business. April's replies showed a strong concentration on the satisfaction gained from keeping order. The customer and customer satisfaction were not included in any of her replies.

b. WHAT ARE YOUR PRODUCTS AND SERVICES?

You can't be in business unless you have a product or service to sell, but have you clearly defined what they are for you and your employees? If you are in the restaurant business, you are obviously selling food, but what else are you selling? Relaxation? Comfort? Self-esteem? Pampering? Quick service? Eye appeal? Tried and true fare or something new and adventurous? Each restaurant is selling food, but each one is also selling other services, depending on the vision of the owners and employees as well as the expectations of the customers.

Ask yourself these questions:

(a) What is your principle product or service?

(b) What other tangible products or services are you selling?

(c) What intangible products or services are you selling?

- Ambiance?

- Pride?

- Self-esteem?

- Dependability?

Make your own list.

You have probably noticed that many commercials and advertisements do not discuss the product, instead they project the image of how you will feel about yourself when driving this particular car, using that particular computer, washing your hair with this shampoo — all intangibles but part of the product or service.

CASE STUDY

When John and Mary asked themselves these questions, they found that while they took pride in the quality of their merchandise, their discussion brought up other considerations — some intangibles that they had overlooked. As a quality boutique they were not selling just shirts or accessories, they were selling pride — pride in looking and dressing well. They were also selling distinctiveness: "You can count on us to always bring you unique, quality merchandise." They were also selling dependability: "You can depend on us to provide you with the products you want and we will stand behind anything we sell."

c. WHO ARE YOUR CUSTOMERS OR CLIENTS?

You may have the best product or service in the world, but the sale is not made until the customer pays for it. Before you went into business, you should have researched your client base so you would know whom to approach to make that sale. It has often been said that when you open a business there are three very important things to consider: location, location, location. But now that you are properly located and in business, you know that there is more to it than that. You need to know everything possible about your customers.

To maximize your business opportunities, ask yourself and your employees these questions:

(a) Who should be buying your products/services?

(b) Why should they be buying your products/services?

(c) Who is buying your products/services?

(d) Why are they buying?

(e) Are you well located to serve your customers?

(f) Are you open the hours to give them service?

(g) What else should you be offering your customers but are not?

(h) Why aren't you offering it, or at least thinking about it?

From the answers to these questions, you can determine if you and your employees agree about the public you should be serving. If you disagree, you need to resolve your customer definition. You may also want to explore the possibilities of attracting a new customer base.

CASE STUDY

When the owners and employees of the ABC Shoppe answered these questions, they found they could easily answer the first six. They were aiming for and getting a clientele of middle- and upper-income customers who bought quality, unique items for themselves or as gifts. The problem came in answering the last two questions. They came to the conclusion that even though their merchandise was good, the location was excellent, and they stayed open at the proper times, they were treating their customers poorly or without courtesy.

When they thought about what they should be offering their customers, but were not, they concluded that they needed to give their customers personal attention and courteous, polite service. They should be demonstrating concern about satisfying the customers, and they should be warm and enthusiastic about their merchandise. After all, if they aren't excited about it, why should the customer be excited? They also decided that they should be developing a friendly, non-threatening climate that would invite people to return.

The answer to the last question was simple, but nobody had taken the time to think about it. The business was new and everybody was so wrapped up in their own responsibilities that unplanned events like brainstorming or creative thinking were pushed on the back burner. Everyone had the attitude "Why think about the store in my own free time?"

d. WHAT DO YOUR CUSTOMERS AND CLIENTS EXPECT?

We keep repeating that a customer relations program is built on expectations, but do you really know what your customers or clients expect from doing business with you? Part of your research should determine those expectations. If you have a steady client base, you can easily mail out a postage-paid reply card asking questions such as the following:

(a) What do you like about our product (or service, store, restaurant, etc.)?

(b) What would you change about our product (or service, etc.)?

(c) Has our customer service been to your satisfaction?

(d) What improvements would you like to see, items changed or added? How can we improve?

(e) Have our employees treated you with respect and courtesy?

(f) How can they be of greater service?

(g) What else can we do to make your work (visit, dining, etc.) easier (better) for you?

Hotels and restaurants often ask customers to fill out a card or the back of the bill regarding service. If you employ this method as a means to gain consumer reaction, be sure to follow through and act upon the comments. Just recently we spent considerable time filling in such a restaurant service enquiry, itemizing the details we thought were important. We filled in the place asking for our telephone number, but we still haven't heard from the restaurant.

If a customer stops doing business with you, you need to find out why. While some dissatisfied people are very vocal, others are not. A non-threatening phone call can get to the heart of the matter. In your research, you should go back over your client list and determine why a customer may have stopped doing business with you.

CASE STUDY

When John and Mary used a reply card to get a sampling of customer reaction, they found customers liked the merchandise and the store itself, but found the service inconsistent. One reply gave details of being rebuked by April, "We would never promise you that." Another pointed out that Jim seemed in a hurry to get the sale over with. A number of replies commented on June's good nature and obvious interest in them, but pointed out that the way she was dressed did not reflect the image of the store. One rather proper respondent added that June's use of slang such as "yeah," "you know," and "okay" detracted from her other good qualities. It was pointed out that there was no gift wrapping provided, yet many customers were buying gifts so this would be a convenient service. Finally, customers noted that when they asked if they could be telephoned when a certain item came in, they were told that the procedure "wasn't store policy."

Ask similar questions of yourself and your staff:

(a) What do you think our customers like about our product (service, store, restaurant, etc.)?

(b) What do you think they would change about our product (service, etc.)?

(c) Do you think our service has been to our customers' satisfaction?

(d) If not, what do you think they would want changed about our service?

(e) Do you think we treat our customers with respect and courtesy?

(f) How could we be of greater service to our customers?

(g) What could we do to make our customers work (visit, dining, etc.) easier, better for them?

(h) Are the telephones being answered politely?

(i) How often and for how long are customers kept on hold?

(j) How many calls are being transferred? How many are lost in transfer?

(k) How many complaints do we receive by telephone daily, weekly, and monthly? What categories do the complaints fall into?

(l) How are complaints by telephone being handled? Who is responsible for handling complaints?

(m) When complaints are resolved, how is this monitored? What is the follow-up to the complaint?

(n) Are any complaints left unresolved?

Once you have discovered your customers' expectations of your products and services, you will need to compare them with yours and those of your employees to see how closely they relate. From the information gathered, you can determine —

(a) status quo,

(b) changes needed,

(c) how to make the changes,

(d) how to put the changes into perspective,

(e) how to monitor new practices,

(f) how to assess results,

(g) how to make adjustments,

(h) how to introduce adjustments,

(i) how to evaluate adjustments,

(j) how to communicate steps to personnel, and

(k) what training is needed.

You can design other questionnaires for other customer contact situations. You may be very surprised at some of the client answers to your questions. We can tell you that cleanliness ranks next to godliness with some customers. That's cleanliness of the physical plant, office, or store, the employees, even the person who makes the deliveries. Make sure that your customer expectations of your company are not being corroded by a subliminal image. Untidy files, unwashed windows, shoes behind doors, out-of-date posters and general untidiness can make a strong impression on people.

An agricultural firm did a survey of their clients and found that the general appearance of their building was having a very negative effect. One reply stated, "How can you be in the business of working with farmers when you have such a healthy growth of pig weed and Russian thistle bordering your property? No self-respecting farmer would tolerate those weeds choking out the grass."

CASE STUDY

When John and Mary looked at the replies from their staff and themselves, they found that Jim believed they were giving the customers good service and could not think of any changes to make. April agreed with him. June felt none of the staff was friendly enough. She also felt that the staff members were sometimes too concerned with the work they were doing (e.g., stocking shelves) and did not give the customer the attention they should. She also brought up the fact that April often corrected her in front of customers or broke in on what she was saying to a customer.

John and Mary didn't think their customers were getting the kind of service they expected and often demanded themselves when they shopped, but they found it difficult to change roles to become service oriented.

e. WHO IS YOUR COMPETITION?

There are hundreds of restaurants in every city. Have you ever wondered why one stays in business for years while scores of others disappear within months? There are now a multitude of computer outlets offering both hardware and software products. Why does one store succeed and another fail when both sell identical products? In many cases, it is because new business owners haven't researched their competition. Never run down a competitor to a customer or client, but be aware of what they are doing right and wrong. Keeping ahead of the competition means learning from their successes and failures. Ask yourself these questions:

(a) How long have they been in business?

(b) What is their reputation for product/service?

(c) What are they doing that we don't do?

(d) Is it attracting more customers/clients for them?

(e) If we are both doing the same thing, how can we do it better?

CASE STUDY

The competition for the ABC Shoppe came from a well-established specialty store eight blocks away. It did not have as great a variety of merchandise and it was not as attractive. However, it did have a regular and steady clientele. The third question — What are they doing that we don't do? — was the important one for John and Mary. They found their competitor's sales staff accommodating and friendly with a focus on serving the customer, even phoning a competing store to find an item if necessary. The store also had a mailing list for special promotions and a customer-pay gift wrapping service.

f. HOW DO YOU RATE RIGHT NOW?

Conduct a customer relations internal/external audit as part of your research.

(a) Are telephones being answered courteously? Is the information that is being given correct? Is the tone of voice warm and friendly? Can you understand the name of the company or is it being "sung" or said so quickly it can't be understood?

(b) Are customers approached with vitality, interest, and enthusiasm, but without aggressive behavior?

(c) Are customers being allowed privacy to make decisions, explore possibilities, and confer with companions?

(d) Are customer complaints and inquiries received in a respectful, agreeable manner and acted upon promptly and efficiently?

(e) Is correspondence answered promptly and in the proper tone?

(f) Are messages taken and handled efficiently and graciously?

(g) Are business facilities well maintained?

(h) Does the staff pay attention to good grooming, decorum, and personal image? Does their personal image reflect the image of the company?

(i) Do staff provide the extra time and attention to make every customer feel special and important to the business?

(j) Are products checked before delivery to make sure they are in proper working order and as specified by the buyer?

(k) Does the product arrive on time and in proper working condition?

(l) Is there follow-up to ensure the customer is satisfied?

(m) Is there follow-up to make sure the customer returns?

(n) Are personnel being told they have done a good job?

Several years ago, we had the opportunity to ride in the
taxi cab of a man who had obviously asked himself all these
questions. The cab was on older model Rolls Royce, immacu-
late inside and out. The driver-owner was equally well
groomed. When we got into the cab, and, yes, he held the
door for us, we found the tiny vases filled with fresh flowers.

Before the cab started, we were asked our destination,
which of the three daily papers we wanted to read, whether
we would prefer a tape of classical, pop, or western music,
silence, or the radio station of our choice. The only other
question was whether we had visited the city before. When
we said we had, but only on business, we were asked if we
had time to take a little swing around some of the more
interesting areas. Suspecting that we would be facing a much
larger fee than the straight ride to the hotel, we hesitated. He
assured us that there would be no extra charge and true to
his word he shut off the meter and took us on a little excursion
through some of the more interesting parts of Toronto. Needless to say, he received a generous tip and was referred to all
our associates.

Here was a man who loved his work, had respect for his
clients, was interested in their welfare, and worked hard to
meet their expectations. But he also worked hard to meet his
own expectations and even though he had been singled out
by customers and journalists for the quality of his business,
he never bought another cab or hired anyone to work for him.
He said he wanted to remain small and in complete control.
He set high expectations for himself, and his reputation

confirmed that quality of service was important to him and, ultimately, to his customers.

CASE STUDY

By performing an audit as discussed above, John and Mary found that there was inconsistency in how the telephone was answered depending on who did the answering. June best conveyed the tone and image they wished, except she used slang. Jim was businesslike, but almost too brisk, and April was sometimes almost hostile.

John and Mary found the three employees were not greeting the customers or offering discreet assistance. They were leaving the customers too much on their own. The maintenance of the store was also inconsistent. Sometimes it opened on time, sometimes it did not. Sometimes the counters were cleaned and tidied, sometimes not. April and Jim were the most consistent in these areas.

There was no follow-through to assure customer satisfaction or to ensure that a customer returned.

Finally, the audit showed that the employees received no monetary or other tangible rewards and verbal praise was sporadic at best.

g. SETTING GOALS

From the information you have gathered, you can confidently set goals for your business. To do so, carefully go though each of the following steps.

(a) Determine why you are in business. Ask not only yourself, but your employees. Do you have the same perceptions? If they differ, why?

(b) Identify clearly what you are offering your clients. Products? Services? (Both the tangible and the intangible.) Once again this a project for both you and your employees. What are the differences between your perceptions and theirs?

(c) Determine who your clients are. Do you and your employees agree? Can you enlarge the client base?

(d) Determine what your clients expect from your products/services.

(e) Determine your competition. Identify their successful and unsuccessful customer/client relations strategies.

(f) Conduct a customer/client relations audit of your company's operating procedures.

(g) Determine the goals for your business or company.

(h) Once your goals have been set, determine the action to achieve the goal.

Use the worksheet shown as Figure #2 on pages 93 and 94 to work out your own goals for your customer relations program.

CASE STUDY

As a result of the surveys, John set up two task forces to establish goals for the store. The first consisted of June and Mary. Their task was to determine ways to better service customers, to attract new customers, and to assure repeated patronage.

John felt that June had the customer's concerns at heart and that Mary had the "shopper's point of view." Mary also had a traveler's knowledge of what other similar stores were doing.

The second task force consisted of Jim and April. Their task was to evaluate present staff skills, determine training needed, and suggest rewards for jobs well done.

By giving Jim and April the staffing goals, John felt he could involve them in an area where both needed help. At the same time, they could capitalize on their obvious skills for creating order and giving attention to detail.

John was not without a task. He set himself up as a committee of one to assure consistency in the day-to-day operation of the store.

The task forces were given paid time to meet and a date was set for reporting to a staff meeting.

In the next chapter, you will see the format the employees at the ABC Shoppe decided was best for them.

FIGURE #2
SETTING GOALS

1. Why are we in business?

My perception	Employee's perceptions	Differences	Why differences?	Goal

2. Services, products (both tangible and intangible)

My perception	Employee's perceptions	Differences	Why differences?	Goal

3. Our customers

My perception	Employee's perceptions	Differences	Why differences?	Goal

4. Customer/client expectations (research)

My perception	Employee's perceptions	Differences	Why differences?	Goal

FIGURE #2 — Continued

5. Competition

Who are they?	What are they doing well?	What mistakes are they making?	What can we do better than them?	Goal
_____	_____	_____	_____	_____
_____	_____	_____	_____	_____
_____	_____	_____	_____	_____

6. Customer/client relations audit

What are we doing well?	What are we doing badly?	What can we change?	What shouldn't we change?	Goal
_____	_____	_____	_____	_____
_____	_____	_____	_____	_____
_____	_____	_____	_____	_____

Goals can be set to —

1. Make employer-employee perceptions the same, achieve a compromise or a new perception.
2. Make customer-employer-employee perceptions the same, achieve a compromise or a new perception.
3. Adapt other business strategies that will improve basic customer relations.
4. Assure that the status of present procedures does not changes.
5. Make present procedures better.
6. Introduce new procedures that will assure better customer service.

8

PUTTING YOUR PLAN TOGETHER

a. PLANNING YOUR SUCCESS

The old adage, "When we fail to plan, we plan to fail," is particularly relevant to customer service. Whether through procrastination, laziness, ignorance, or indifference, if we ignore the planning process today, we are laying the foundation for failure tomorrow.

Let's assume that ignorance is the major culprit, and the majority of us are unfamiliar with planning — particularly a new venture. The first questions that surface are, Where do I begin? and, What are the precedents to guide me? It's this stage of planning, taking the first wobbly steps, that can be most daunting.

We could contemplate it more, but like other business people, the more we dwell on the problem, the larger it looms, and any problem can quickly assume mammoth proportions, even creating second thoughts about the wisdom of venturing into unfamiliar territory.

b. BITE-SIZED CHUNKS: DEVELOPING TASK FORCES

The solution is to cut it down to size, preferably into chunks, that can be understood, accepted, and assimilated. Much like golf, no seasoned player would expect a hole-in-one on a 400-yard fairway. Instead, he or she would plan a series of approach shots, using different clubs to suit the terrain and the distance the ball is required to travel. Using this system, the golfer concentrates on the immediate shot, using the driver or iron most appropriate for the approach rather than filling the mind with fanciful images of the putter when the green is the size of a dime on the horizon. First things first, sums it up aptly.

Developing a plan for customer relations has to be done logically and in an orderly manner, and yet, like golf, it can be frustrating, unpredictable, and sometimes wearying. But the elation that comes from a winning strategy and consistently better performance makes it all worthwhile.

Setting up task forces can be a useful means to organizing the various facets of your plan. If you decide to use this method, follow these steps to guide your task forces:

(a) Determine the need for a task force

- Do you want input from all personnel?

- Do you want a consensus of opinion?

- Do you want commitment to the proposal of a customer relations program?

If you answer yes to these questions, then establish a task force.

(b) Determine the objective for the task force

- What do you want it to accomplish?

- Do not give it too many topics or too broad a mandate to cover. You may need more than one task force.

(c) Determine the responsibilities of the task force

- What is the agenda for the task force?

- What is expected of the task force? For example, if the task force is to determine the customers' perception of the company, will it devise methods of research, implement the research, evaluate the research, support the status quo, or bring about change?

(d) Determine reporting strategy

- At what point(s) in its agenda does the task force report back to the planning committee? Set a time frame for interim and final reporting.

(e) Determine the makeup and numbers of the task force

- Ensure that there is representation from all areas immediately concerned by the agenda.

- Ensure there is representation from all areas affected by the agenda over a period of time.

- Keep to workable numbers to allow for maximum discussion.

(f) Select a chair for the task force

- Someone may volunteer to chair or a chair can be appointed or selected by the committee itself and can be anyone from the loading dock to the front desk. (For more information on meeting formats and guidelines, see *The Business Guide to Effective Speaking*, and *Chairing a Meeting with Confidence*, two other titles in the Self-Counsel Series.)

(g) Develop a work plan for the task force

- A work plan can be developed by the task force itself or by working in conjunction with a program development leader.

- Identify objective of task force.

- Identify steps to reach objective.

- Put steps in order of importance.

- Establish a time frame for reaching the objective.

- Establish a time frame for completing each step.

- Allocate responsibilities.

- Establish a regular schedule of routine meetings.

- Gain commitment from all concerned.

c. A FOUNDATION FOR PLANNING

In chapter 6, we used a flowchart to show how to develop a program for your organization. One section of that flowchart was on planning the program, which covered five major areas.

In planning your program, you may decide you need more than five areas or you may discover you can combine some areas under one heading. There is no hard and fast rule. The criterion is whatever is best for your organization at this time.

d. THE EASY, STEP-BY-STEP PLAN

Obviously the first draft will not be a perfect plan, nor will it be the most comprehensive, but it will get you started on the planning activity. In the process, you will overcome the mental block that often arises when you face something for the first time.

So let's work through the planning process together. Go through the following questions and note your answers on a piece of paper. As you work your way down the list, you will see signposts emerge — conclusions that will point you in the right direction, letting you know what is needed, what would be nice to have, and what you should discard.

Because this type of planning process may be new to you, we want to be sure to capture your undivided attention for about 10 minutes. Here is what to do:

(a) Arrange to have all your telephone calls intercepted.

(b) Close your office door.

(c) Take two to three minutes to sweep out the mental debris.

(d) Take a deep breath, grab a pencil, and go!

Let's start with some very basic questions to get you in the right frame of mind.

(a) Why are you even considering a customer relations program?

(b) Why is it essential to your organization?

(c) What do you wish to accomplish?

(d) Are your objectives realistic?

(e) What do you stand to gain?

(f) What do you stand to lose?

(g) Are you willing to commit money to the program?

(h) Do your competitors have a program in place?

(i) What do you admire about their programs?

(j) Are there segments you would wish to plagiarize?

This isn't a complete list. You can add questions of your own, and the more questions you ask, the more you will learn about your organization and your competitors.

The answers you have written down can now be contemplated, verified, then polished, and quickly adopted as your objectives. Once you have cleaned up the prose, you may discover you want to change parts, which is perfectly acceptable. You may even want to rip the whole thing up and start again, and this is all right too. If you are changing the plan, it means you are thinking about it, and we couldn't ask for anything more.

So remember, your plan is not inscribed in stone...it's a flexible tool to help you recognize some business realities and to guide you in preparing for those realities. With a good grasp of where you want to go and why you need to go there, next you need to consider the facts about your customers and clients.

e. WHOM ARE YOU TRYING TO REACH?

Your research completed in chapter 6 told you quite a lot about the people who are important to your organization: employees, customers, clients, shareholders, suppliers, and, often, government agencies. Now you need to put a priority on the different groups (for ease of operation) and decide which objectives apply to each. Some objectives may apply only to a limited number of people, while some objectives may be relevant to all groups. It's like mixing and matching your wardrobe. A navy blue jacket can complement light gray slacks in addition to light blue slacks or tan slacks. According to the occasion, you choose one in preference to the other depending on how you wish to appear, what impression you wish to create, and your perception of the group's expectations.

If this principle sounds familiar, it's because you read it in an earlier chapter when we were talking about knowing your organization's image and reputation.

f. BREAKING DOWN THE PLAN

Once you have sliced your research and questions into bite-sized chunks, you then need to slice your plan in a similar fashion — into short-, medium- and long-range goals. It is your plan, so you decide what short-term means to you. It could be one month, one quarter, six months, or a year. It could also be five years for well-established organizations where tradition dictates that change be minimal and gradual.

A useful model that we will use in this book is defining a short range as one year, medium range as three years, and anything five years or more as long range.

In developing your one-year plan, your planning committee or task force should follow these steps:

(a) Determine your organization's weaknesses and potential irritants.

100

(b) Decide on present strengths and virtues you desire to encourage and add.

(c) Make a commitment to change.

(d) Create and establish a structure that will make the changes more acceptable and easier to implement.

(e) Design clear and precise standards so everyone understands the lines of authority, decision-making powers, and guidelines for behavior.

(f) Develop a system to monitor and evaluate performance. People need to know how well they are doing.

(g) Give top priority to training. Don't assume people will embrace your plans with joy until they understand them and, more important, understand their role in them.

(h) Communicate the progress, or lack of it, continually. Sporadic announcements will receive short shrift. Communication is going to be a major tool in your customer relations program, so why not set an example; show them how to use it, don't just tell them how.

(i) Develop enthusiasm for both the concept and the program. Enthusiasm is contagious. If you don't get wound up about the program possibilities, why should anybody else? The way to develop enthusiasm is by encouraging pride — pride in who a person is, where he or she works, and what he or she produces. Pride is an intangible but powerful ally. We are all familiar with people who exude pride in themselves and their work. They seem to glow and sparkle, and they are literally walking ambassadors for their organizations. With proper encouragement, your people could sparkle and glow considerably brighter.

101

(j) Determine the rewards for achieving goals and objectives. Announce how the recognition or award will be handled or shared. Also be prepared to recognize outstanding performance by individuals or groups. Again, remind all employees that this is their plan, and it will work only if each takes a personal interest in making it successful.

g. WHO IS GOING TO DO WHAT?

Now you need to bring together all the bits and pieces of paper you have been shuffling and put some names and time frames on them. This is necessary to get people involved and also to get the work done. As an example, Sample #2 shows how one business outlined steps in their recognition/reward system. This type of outline works well for segments of the plan, but for the total plan you need to develop a critical path or time table (see Sample #3). Use whatever works best for you.

As the pieces of the puzzle start to slip into place, we can tentatively put target dates for implementation of program segments on the calendar or critical path (see Sample #4).

SAMPLE #2
REWARD/RECOGNITION PROGRAM

Committee members	Action needed	Date required	Assigned to	Reporting method
J.D. B.T. F.B. R.H. J.K.	Researching rewards at ABC Inc.	July 10/9-	B.T. & J.K.	Memo & phone
	Develop monitoring system	Aug. 4/9-	R.H.	Memo Aug. 1 followed by meeting Aug. 5

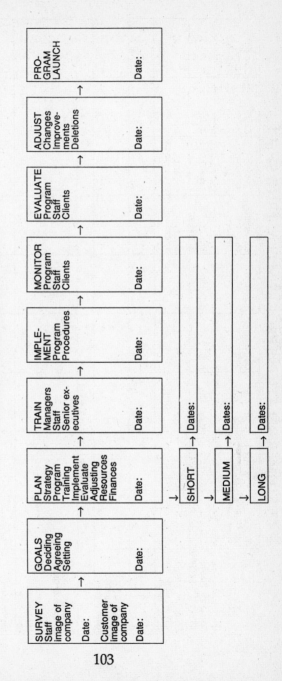

SAMPLE #3
TASK FORCE TIME TABLE

SURVEY Staff image of company	GOALS Deciding Agreeing Setting	PLAN Strategy Program Training Implement Evaluate Adjusting Resources Finances	TRAIN Managers Staff Senior executives	IMPLE- MENT Program Procedures	MONITOR Program Staff Clients	EVALUATE Program Staff Clients	ADJUST Changes Improve- ments Deletions	PRO- GRAM LAUNCH
Date:	Date:	Date:	Date:	Date:	Date:	Date:	Date:	Date:
Customer image of company								
Date:								

SHORT → Dates:

MEDIUM → Dates:

LONG → Dates:

SAMPLE #4
CUSTOMER RELATIONS PROGRAM PLANNING SHEET

	Who is responsible?	How will it be done?	Start date	Completion date	Approval	Communication methods	Specific concerns	Skill training	Cost (include release time)
Company image survey: Personnel	J.D.	Staff meeting	May 1	May 30	M.D.	Staff meeting	Morale	J.S.	
Company image survey: Customer/client	M.S.	Mail	May 1	June 15	M.D.	Staff meeting	Repeat customers	L.M.	
Setting goals									
Planning procedures to meet goals			*Put on program training here						
Implementing procedures to meet goals Short-term Medium-term Long-term									
Monitoring procedures									
Evaluating procedures									
Adjusting procedures									

h. REVIEW YOUR PLAN

Just about this time you need to pause, step back, and consider what you have accomplished so far. Does it make sense? Is it realistic? Is it what you want?

If the answers are yes, then you need to ask yourself if the plan is put into operation will it affect your quality of service in a negative manner? In other words, will you spend more time fulfilling the plan than in providing quality service to your customers?

Will your service be as good as before, or better, while still being dependable, consistent, time conscious and economical? If the answer comes out yes again, then it's time to buy a large roll of white paper from the stationery suppliers (the type used to cover tables at barbecues), pin a generous length on the wall, and start tracking or developing a king-sized critical path. At this juncture it's relatively simple.

First, at the right edge of the paper write in your implementation date. Next, start working backward slotting in people, activities, time requirements, and deadlines as agreed. The beauty of a big chart is that everybody is aware of it. But even more significant is that people tend to respond more readily when they realize their names, assignments, and completion dates are on public view.

Once you have mastered the one-year plan, repeat the process for the three- and five-year plans. You will find it develops more quickly as the players benefit from the experience of the one-year planning exercise.

i. SUMMARY

In summary, break the large challenge into a series of smaller, more manageable challenges. Start the process now. Procrastination will make it appear more difficult than it really is. Do it one step at a time. Familiarize yourself with your organization's service in relation to your customers' needs.

Don't try to make a perfect plan. Be willing to scrap it and start over again. It's not wasted time but a valuable learning opportunity, and it lets you acknowledge there could be frills you don't need. Be sure of the impression you wish to develop or enhance. Make certain it's appropriate to you and that you can maintain and improve it indefinitely. Create a workable structure that will ease any change that's necessary. Make sure the program belongs to everybody and everybody is kept informed on progress.

Don't forget encouragement. It's the salve for the bruised ego, the vitamin for the tired committee member, and the elixir for continuing success in business.

Share the work, share the accolades, keep to deadlines, keep moving forward.

Unplanned systems operate for the convenience of the organization. Planned systems are for the benefit of customers, clients, and employees. So planning means knowing where you are going and when you expect to arrive. By asking questions, you can develop a customized road map that will chart your intended progress and measure how successful you have been.

CASE STUDY

When the staff meeting was held at the ABC Shoppe, everyone was enthusiastic about the results of their discussions, and a certain pride was evident when they talked about their "fact finding" endeavors. Mary and June offered the following suggestions for improving service to present customers and for attracting new customers:

(a) All customers should be treated as welcome guests with warmth, smiles, and greetings.

(b) Customers should be offered assistance respectfully and should not be harassed or pushed.

(c) If asked for gift suggestions, the salesperson must take the time to be helpful and offer a range of merchandise at varying prices.

(d) New, elegant packaging should be designed and used in a way that would make gift wrapping easy without any additional charge to the customers. Samples and prices were shown.

(e) Customers should be asked if they cared to be placed on a mailing list for upcoming sales and special promotions.

(f) When an item is out of stock, the customer should be asked if he or she wants to be advised when a new shipment comes in. Names and telephone numbers should be entered in a book kept at the sales counter.

(g) Customers, whether they purchase anything or not, should be given a prepaid postcard questionnaire asking for suggestions for better service and ideas for new merchandise. When returned, the postcard should be kept on file and the customer should receive a 10% discount on the next purchase.

(h) Advertising and special promotions should coincide. For example, on Mother's Day, a free carnation could be given with every purchase.

(i) Mints, placed in small candy dishes at the front of the store, should be offered to all customers.

(j) Appropriate music should be used as an unobtrusive background.

(k) New marketing ideas should be suggested monthly by employees. When an idea is used, the employee who suggested it should be suitably rewarded.

(l) The customer must be given full, discreet attention. When a customer enters the store, the employees must stop doing whatever they are busy with and help the customer.

(m) All staff, regardless of title, must treat each other with respect.

(n) A shopper's service for people who cannot do their own shopping should be implemented. The store could keep on file details about preferences of price range, individual taste in colors and styles, and the selection, gift wrapping, and delivery would be provided at no extra charge.

(o) A gift suggestion catalogue should be mailed to businesses in the area promoting the shopper's service for retirement gifts or personalized recognition awards.

(p) A calendar of special days should be kept for busy customers to remind them in advance of birthdays and anniversaries. The reminder could include sizes, special requirements, and a tasteful list of suggestions.

(q) Flowers could be ordered as an added service (from the shop next door) and unusual gifts could be suggested. While these would not represent direct sales of merchandise, each transaction would build trust between the customer and the store and would establish the dependability of the store for assistance with a variety of needs.

Mary and June summarized by noting that it is important to measure the responses to flyers, catalogues, special days, and special events so that they know what works and what doesn't. A simple question to the customer, "How did you find out about our special?" would provide the answer, which must be recorded to provide a meaningful measurement of responses.

Jim and April, as predicted, came up with a detailed plan for employee evaluation and training. Using the responses from customers, employers, and employees, they were able to complete the plan. It is shown in Sample #5.

John's report consisted of the need for a checklist for opening the store. He presented part of it and asked for contributions from the staff. It took shape along these lines:

(a) Arrive no later than 8:30 a.m. Store must be opened promptly at 9:00 a.m.

(b) Before store is opened —

- turn on all lights,
- clean counter, window, and mirrors,
- tidy displays, and
- count cash float.

There was also a checklist for the person who closed the store, another for dealing with suppliers, marking and pricing, and stocking the shelves.

The result of the task forces was the evolution of a customer service program that kept the focus firmly on the customer. It began with an orderly, logical way of doing business and a demonstrated concern for personnel development, and it provided the foundation for a continuing program to better serve the customers. Best of all, because everyone had been involved and each had contributed, it become "our" plan for "our" store.

The results of the task forces and surveys showed a definite need for training and employee recognition, plus some role changes for everyone but June, who continued in her job as clerk.

Mary gave her bookkeeping chores to Jim and took over one of his evenings and some of his Saturdays in the store. This gave her some first-hand ideas about what customers wanted in the way of merchandise and helped her buy stock with customers' preferences in mind.

April took the responsibilities of dealing with the suppliers, pricing inventory, and arranging displays. John, alone, would be the boss.

Samples #6 and #7 show the planning and implementation process for the ABC Shoppe.

SAMPLE #5
THE ABC CUSTOMER RELATIONS PROGRAM SKILL EVALUATION

To be filled in by *all* employees – (designed by Jim and April)

STAFF	AREAS FOR IMPROVEMENT	AREAS OF STRENGTH	POTENTIAL VIRTUES	APPEARANCE AND BEHAVIOR GUIDLINES
JOHN	Managerial skills Getting used to authority Negotiating skills Understanding of publicity	People skills Enthusiasm Attention to detail Dependable	Motivational skills Positive attitude Leadership qualities	Must look like leader Must act like leader Must dress like leader
MARY	Not sales oriented Too consumer-oriented Unused to business conver- sation Never had to promote business	Good buying instincts Has people skills Confident in abilities	Objective view of staff Analytical view of business Orderly mind for long-range planning	Good appearance Looks successful Needs to develop confidence in skills
JUNE	Poor "dress" image Student Almost too popular Too much "slang"	Good personality, warm and friendly; seems genuinely interested in customers Outgoing, enthusiastic Willing to learn	Friendliness could encourage customers to return if proper relationship established Attracts young clientele	Dress unacceptable Needs advice on clothing and language
JIM	Almost too businesslike Uses a minimum of words and appears abrupt Shyness is part of problem	Good, methodical mind Persistent Works hard Has good business background	Bookeeping skills could be utilized more often Could be valuable in dealing with senior execs or business organizations	Dresses rather stodgy, although good quality Needs more modern wardrobe attitude
APRIL	Brusque with customers Defensive, fault-finding Poor people skills	Excellent displays Thorough in marking and stocking A lot of determination Appropriate dress	Artistic talent a big plus in attracting clients May have skills in haut couture not realized	Appearance is good, but dealings with customers poor Etiquette needs work

SAMPLE #5 — Continued

STAFF	DESIRED STANDARDS	PERFORMANCE EVALUATION	REWARDS AVAILABLE	TRAINING NEEDED
JOHN	To be a leader Exhibit confidence Encourage others Make sound decisions		Increased income from more successful store	Leadership skills Managing people Strategic planning Promotion and publicity
MARY	To be able to fill in as boss and exhibit managerial skills as well as sales skills		Increased income from more successful store	Sales training Some leadership skills
JUNE	Personal goals are set in conjunction with Mary then by John	Evaluated initially by Mary then reviewed by John	Rewards should be equally available to all employees: • A profit-sharing plan • Monetary rewards for achieving sales goals • Suggestion box — if used • Cost-cutting ideas • Labor-saving ideas	Sales training Image awareness Etiquette training
JIM	Personal goals are set in conjunction with Mary then approved by John	Evaluated initially by Mary then reviewed by John		Sales training Image awareness Confidence building Etiquette training
APRIL	Personal goals are set in conjunction with Mary then approved by John	Evaluated initially by Mary then reviewed by John		Sales training Image awareness Communication skills Courtesy and politeness

SAMPLE #6
THE ABC CUSTOMER RELATIONS PROGRAM PLANNING FLOWCHART

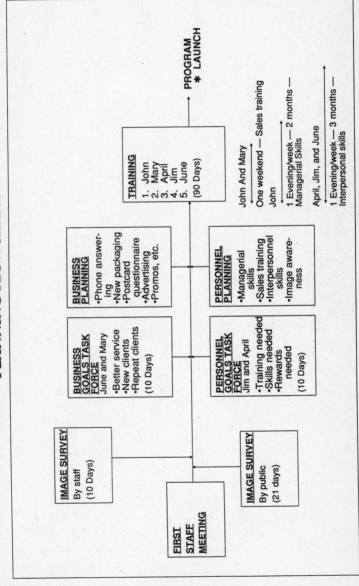

SAMPLE # 7
THE ABC CUSTOMER RELATIONS PROGRAM
IMPLEMENTATION PROCESS

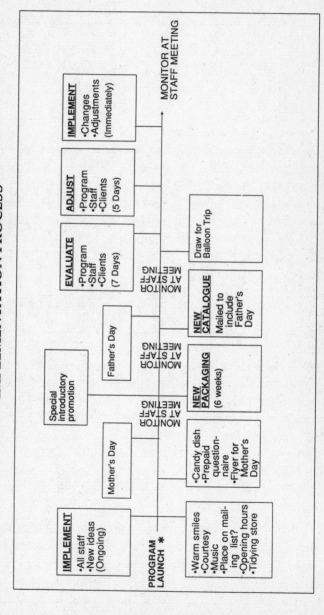

9

COMMUNICATING YOUR CUSTOMER RELATIONS PROGRAM TO YOUR EMPLOYEES

Good customer relations begins with good employee relations. Both you and your staff must be sold on the program; as managers and supervisors know, you get work done through your staff. Being able to communicate effectively with employees can mean the difference between the success or failure of your customer relations program and, ultimately, your business. Throughout this book, we've emphasized communication as being always important to the plan. Now it is time to be specific.

a. COMMUNICATING WITH EMPLOYEES

Sometimes we pay too much attention to the way we communicate, and not enough to content and purpose. We become engrossed with memos and meetings, forgetting that communication is taking place all the time during every minute of the job. Good communication cannot be switched on and off at somebody's whim. Nor is communication a placebo or gimmick to be used at a time of crisis or when promoting a new program. Good communication is the heart of any business, the most important tool for getting things done. It is the basis for understanding, for cooperation, for action...and for profit.

Communicating with your staff is not accomplished by words alone. Tone of voice, facial expressions, the set of the shoulders, the lift of an eyebrow — all send a message that is read by employees. Even silence sends a message; we can all

115

recall the words that were not said, either in praise or rebuke. An owner, manager, or supervisor casts a long shadow; each word or action is larger than life to an employee. The employee, whether reacting or emulating, in turn casts a shadow on the customer or client.

b. ESSENTIALS OF GOOD EMPLOYEE COMMUNICATION

Communication is a journey, not a destination. It isn't the single step of transmitting an idea — telling someone. Good communication begins with listening — being sincerely concerned about people and their problems and becoming enthusiastic about their ideas.

The second step in good communication is thinking through and clarifying an idea in your own mind, then with the help of others, setting a purpose for the communication. The third step is to share the idea with the people who will carry it out, and the fourth step is to share your enthusiasm for the idea and get your people energized to take the action that will fulfill the purpose of the communication. The final step is follow-through; you need to monitor the process, and the results, to see if the action is ongoing and unchanging.

Let's take a look at those steps and see if they tie into your customer relations program.

1. Listening

Your listening began when you asked for input from your employees. You listened carefully to their concerns and their ideas for the program. You took what they had to say seriously, sometimes adapting your own ideas when you realized that theirs made more sense.

2. Purpose

Having taken into consideration the company's objectives, your own goals, and the input from your employees, you have built a customer relations program. Your purpose is to convince the employees to put the program into practice and make it work.

3. Communicating the idea

This step is not as simple as it may seem. The message must be sent in a language that employees can understand. Too often employee reaction to a "state-of-the-union" message by the company president is, What was that all about? The message has not been delivered in language that the audience understands or relates to, or the message is not complete.

A whole department in a Calgary-based oil company became disgruntled when the company moved into a new multi-million dollar building. The department's perception was that it was getting less space than in the old building. In fact, they were getting more space. Someone neglected to tell them that they had additional storage space on another floor. Less space translated into loss of prestige. The ensuing dissatisfaction was expressed in a work-to-rule attitude that became so evident the company president got involved and started an inquiry into the problem.

Good communicators keep their antennas tuned in. They develop a sensitivity to both the viewpoint and the level of comprehension of their staff. They realize an employee receives a message, whether written or verbal, and thinks How will this affect me? Does it mean more or less money? More work? A change in status? Longer hours?

Before you talk with your staff about your new customer relations program, be sure you think through your method of communicating. Think through, too, how they will react to your proposal.

4. Motivating personnel

Not only must you have a purpose for your communication, be sensitive to your personnel, and express your ideas with clarity, but you must also encourage your people to accept the new ideas, and then act on them. Employees respond better when they know what is expected of them, when they learn about change before it takes place, and when they feel free to discuss problems with supervisors. When they believe they are an important part of the organization, they will work with greater interest and enthusiasm. It's the working and communicating relationship between management, supervisors, and employees on a daily basis that builds a team. As trust develops, the quality of the working-communicating relationship improves and, in turn, motivates that team. Motivation comes from within. Neither flowery speeches nor negative haranguing will motivate personnel.

A store manager addressed his staff by bawling them out for an hour and a half. He called them down for their past performance, made comparisons between staff members, and generally painted a black picture of the retail business in general. He concluded with threats of firing if sales did not improve. Then he asked for questions and comments. A newly hired employee spoke: "You have certainly given us all the negatives of the business. Are there any good reasons why we should be working in this business, and particularly for you?" The manager was dumbfounded by the question and could not think of one positive thing to say. The outcome was that three employees quit. Customers were confronted by either fearful or defensive sales staff and sales did not go up. The store manager had not created a positively motivated team. He did not listen, he did not inspire, he did not set a good example.

Employees see economic benefits, more money, and more security as reasons to do a good job. But they desperately need recognition for a job well done plus a measure of personal job satisfaction. They need the regard of managers and supervisors along with fellow employees. Many would like the opportunity to take on more responsibility. When you present your customer relations plan to your employees, be aware that encouragement is a vehicle that will motivate

118

them, so they can plan their part in the program willingly and with purpose.

5. Following through

Telling personnel about your customer relations plan is just the beginning. Every communication must have a follow-through. Your well-thought-out plan has steps that need to be followed in sequence. Each step has a monitoring point to see that the agreed procedure has been followed, and is built into the plan. The prime consideration is making sure that your staff completely understands the plan. You must ensure that all the steps and evaluations take place just as outlined. As in the game of golf, if there is no follow-through in your swing, your plan will start to go off course.

c. COMMUNICATION MUST BE CONSTANT

In the long run, employees are motivated by what management does, not by what it says. Nobody is fooled by the manager who suddenly becomes concerned over your health or your son's baseball team when previously a grunt was all you got in reply to your "good morning." Communication grows in a climate of trust and confidence. The supervisor-manager who keeps promises, reports facts honestly, and listens sincerely does not have to fall back on phony good fellowship. Before you "sell" your customer relations program to your staff, assess your own communication skills and make a determined effort to upgrade those that need polishing, particularly if you expect your message to be understood, accepted, and properly introduced.

Ask yourself these questions:

(a) If I make a promise, do I follow through?

(b) If I am asked for help or information, do I listen and respond sincerely, without sarcasm or criticism?

119

(c) If I ask for input, do I listen with genuine interest and use the input whenever possible?

(d) Do I credit the person's input?

(e) Do I give praise when it is due? (But not use insincere flattery to create good will?)

(f) Do I ask questions when I don't understand?

(g) Do I stimulate people to ask questions and express their ideas?

If you can answer yes to these questions, then it's time to launch your customer relations plan with your staff. But if you have not created a good communications climate, it's critical you spend some time doing so before you present your plan. (You may wish to have others evaluate you using the above questions. Sometimes a person's own perception is biased.)

CASE STUDY

From the surveys, John found that he was a good listener. As a journalist, he was trained to gather information. Mary, as a dentist, usually spent time with people who had their mouths full of cotton. She was used to telling patients what to do and found she was an impatient listener wanting to "get on with it."

As professionals, both worked hard at keeping their promises and were used to meeting deadlines. They found themselves weak when it came to giving praise. As strong individuals often working alone, they did not expect or need a great deal of praise themselves.

It was also a revelation when they realized that rarely had they asked for input from the staff. The staff concurred with their self-evaluation.

With the decision that the store should have only one boss, and that should be John, who spent more time in the store than Mary, the answers helped them make a conscious decision to keep their partnership discussions away from the store.

d. GETTING YOUR IDEAS ACROSS

Getting ideas across makes up more than 50% of the working day of executives, managers, and supervisors. Hicks B. Waldron, Chairman and CEO of Avon Products Inc., says that he spends 60% of his time communicating. The largest part of that time is communicating to employees ranging from hourly workers to senior managers. His communication is aimed at rallying employees to support company plans in order to improve business.

When you present new ideas to employees, present them in small chunks and in simple language. Decide beforehand what your thrust is. In the case of your customer relations communication, it is the whole plan. The second thing to decide is what the main parts of the plan are and, finally, what details the staff need to understand the whole idea. Often, too many details are presented too soon, which can confuse everyone. Be patient with the listener who is slow to grasp your points. Take time to explain, but not at the expense of others. Offer to discuss their concerns on an individual basis.

e. ORDERS

Orders differ from ideas. Ideas can prompt discussion and can be changed. An order is given to bring about certain results. Orders can fall into three general classifications:

(a) The implied order or suggestion that somethin' needs to be done but leaves the doer to go ahead his or her own initiative

(b) The request — a mild, tactful form of orde' would you like to..." or "I wonder if you '

(c) The direct, straightforward comman' "Don't do that."

121

decision to keep their partnership discussions away from the store.

d. GETTING YOUR IDEAS ACROSS

Getting ideas across makes up more than 50% of the working day of executives, managers, and supervisors. Hicks B. Waldron, Chairman and CEO of Avon Products Inc., says that he spends 60% of his time communicating. The largest part of that time is communicating to employees ranging from hourly workers to senior managers. His communication is aimed at rallying employees to support company plans in order to improve business.

When you present new ideas to employees, present them in small chunks and in simple language. Decide beforehand what your thrust is. In the case of your customer relations communication, it is the whole plan. The second thing to decide is what the main parts of the plan are and, finally, what details the staff need to understand the whole idea. Often, too many details are presented too soon, which can confuse everyone. Be patient with the listener who is slow to grasp your points. Take time to explain, but not at the expense of others. Offer to discuss their concerns on an individual basis.

e. ORDERS

Orders differ from ideas. Ideas can prompt discussion and can be changed. An order is given to bring about certain results. Orders can fall into three general classifications:

(a) The implied order or suggestion that something needs to be done but leaves the doer to go ahead on his or her own initiative

(b) The request — a mild, tactful form of order. "How would you like to..." or "I wonder if you would...."

(c) The direct, straightforward command: "Do this," "Don't do that."

A request does not offend the sensitive worker. The first time an error is made, a request to correct it maintains the friendliness that keeps the employee on your side. The direct command may have to be used if the error is repeated. An emergency is another occasion that usually requires a direct command, which when used infrequently, stands out emphatically.

The presentation of your customer relations program should not be an order. If your plan has been conceived with proper input from your staff, the presentation should prompt discussion but require little change.

You may find, however, that as the plan goes into practice and becomes a concrete policy, you may want strict adherence to it. Reminders, requests, and suggestions should be used before resorting to orders. Orders should be given in private if possible. They may be necessary to avert a crisis or to shock workers and ultimately save them from dismissal.

1. **Requisites for giving orders**

(a) The employee receiving the order must have the training, skill, and physical ability to carry out the order satisfactorily.

(b) The employee should understand how the order fits into the total context.

(c) The employee should carry out the order willingly. This is usually the direct result of the manner, including tone of voice, in which the order is given.

(d) The order should be made important in the mind of the employees carrying it out. Orders, suggestions, or requests that are merely "thrown out" will be carried out in the same manner.

(e) Make an order perfectly clear: what the employee is to do, how it is to be done, when it is to be done, and the result expected. Speak the language the employee understands. Remember, just because the employee nods in agreement does not mean the message has been understood.

2. Giving orders

(a) Point out the facts or conditions that have made the order necessary. You want to dispel any impression that the order is a personal reprimand.

(b) State the results expected.

(c) Thoroughly understand the job to be done.

(d) Assign work to the proper employee.

(e) Give the orders clearly, concisely, and distinctly.

(f) Don't assume the orders are understood; be sure they are understood. Ask for feedback.

(g) Avoid sarcasm and profanity.

(h) Do not give an order in anger.

(i) If possible, demonstrate.

(j) Do not give too many orders at one time.

(k) Give orders through proper channels. Do not bypass an immediate supervisor to order an employee.

(l) Some orders should be written down. Directions and company policies are good examples. Keep the language simple. For example, saying "Refrain from engaging" instead of "don't" is a waste of words.

(m) Follow through. Check back to be sure that the employee has understood and is performing the order satisfactorily.

(n) Praise sincerely when it is due.

f. REPRIMANDING

Good customer relations must be consistent. If an employee communicates negatively with clients and customers, immediate action is needed by the manager or supervisor to communicate the problem to the staff member and to change behavior. Once your customer relations plan has been communicated to your employees, accepted by them, and in place, it must be operational at all times. One non-performing employee can undermine the whole program.

Before you reprimand, get all the facts first. The customer who reports poor service may be a constant complainer. Know your employees well. If you have created the right working atmosphere with employees who are conscientious, you know they take pride in their jobs and in their company.

Never lose your temper and bawl out an employee and never reprimand an employee in front of others. You only lose your own credibility. Keep your composure and logically discuss the problem and the consequences of the employee's actions.

Listen carefully and calmly. Ask what could have caused the incident: worry? indifference? health? misunderstanding? resentment? no commitment to the program? Use a sympathetic, interested approach. Don't let prejudice or bias interfere with the process.

The employee should understand what the problem is, how he or she created the problem, what the consequences are, what is to be done, and what to expect if the problem occurs again. Make the employee understand what effect the incident has on the company, on fellow employees, and on him or her.

Get the employee to take responsibility for his or her future conduct. You want a loyal, enthusiastic, dependable employee willing to cooperate and make your customer relations plan work.

g. SUMMARY

(a) Listen to your employees, both when planning and communicating the program and at every step of its implementation:

- Make the physical setting conducive to good listening. Make it private and get rid of distractions like ringing phones and curious onlookers.

- Face the person squarely so you can take in not only what they are saying, but how they are saying it.

- Rid yourself of bias and prejudice.

- If the person is reluctant to talk, ask questions. Express what you feel. Find out if they share the same opinion.

- Interrupt sparingly. Do not contradict.

- Do not lose your temper. Hear the other person out.

- If the other person loses his or her temper, let him or her talk and defuse.

- Listen for ideas and underlying feelings.

- Consider the other person's point of view.

- Evaluate fairly the logic and credibility of what you hear.

- Do not feel you must have the last word.

(b) When you present your customer relations plan, set goals:

- Set your immediate goal.

- Set your long-term goals.

- Break down your information into small pieces. Use only as much detail as is necessary.

(c) Know your employees:

- What is their present attitude toward work, the company, yourself?

- What do they expect from you?

- Will they see the plan as something worthwhile to themselves, or only something worthwhile to you?

(d) Know yourself: If your communication habits are bad, you should be implementing change before you present your plan. If necessary, take a course or get some individual coaching. You want to sell your plan and be credible.

(e) Plan your approach:

- Choose the right time. You may wish to conform to the custom of meeting Monday morning, or you may wish to make the presentation of the plan a very special event. Once again, be aware of employees' sensibilities. Don't keep them in the dark. One large company made it a practice to fire personnel after they had returned from vacation. It got so that no one would take their scheduled vacation period because they were afraid they would be without a job on return. Let employees know what the meeting is about and that it is good news.

- Consult with others. Keep an ongoing dialogue with those who played an active part in the planning process. Get them involved in the presentation of the plan.

- Choose a location with the right atmosphere.

- Be natural but serious in your delivery style. Judge their reaction to a positive or negative approach: "We've got real trouble with our customer services" or "We've got the answer to our customer relations problem."

126

- Keep it simple. Don't try to discuss too much at one time. Speak in language everyone understands.

- Allow for discussion.

- Answer questions clearly.

- Follow through. Have procedures that will get the plan off and running and use them. Have a method of evaluating long-term procedures at various points. Evaluate the success of the procedures at appropriate conclusions.

- Be prepared to give credit.

- Be prepared to turn your plan into policy, policy into procedure, and procedure into orders.

- Be prepared to reward or reprimand, fairly.

CASE STUDY

At the ABC Shoppe, John and Mary were able to build a team by truly participating in the staff meetings and in the task forces, and by really listening and responding to their staff.

John found that he usually only had to request, or even suggest, a point, and soon the work was done. Only on one occasion did he have to reprimand. April had just finished putting together a very attractive display when a customer removed the cashmere sweater to have a better look at it. April, feeling miffed, her masterpiece having been dismantled, told the customer not to touch the display. John made light of the moment and while the customer did not buy that particular sweater, she bought another. In the privacy of his office, John reminded April that while she had to redo the display, she should keep in mind that the objective was to sell the merchandise. He also reminded her that she would be sharing in the commission from the sale.

10
TRAINING EMPLOYEES

We said in chapter 1 that a problem with customer service is that employees are not encouraged to think nor are they trained for responsibility. To ensure the success of your customer relations program, make sure all employees feel they have a stake in its success. Find ways to get them involved and enthused. Remind them that this is their program.

Once you have agreed on the objectives for your program, it's a good idea to include training in your plans. Telephone answering techniques, sales procedures, dress, and decorum may need sprucing up, so include them from the outset.

You can organize and present the training program yourself or use consultants. Either way it's important that training not be confused with function. Keep it separate from regularly scheduled work.

Training must not be used to evaluate an employee's work performance. Imagine our dismay on finding a supervisor in one of our training workshops using the performance of participants as part of their job evaluation. Imagine, also, the participants' reaction if they knew they were being evaluated while struggling to master new and unfamiliar skills. Obviously they would recoil from being involved. Your employees would react in a similar manner and your whole customer relations program could be stranded before it even has a chance to get airborne. Let us repeat: Do not use the learning process as foundation for job appraisal. Later, as the workers become more comfortable with the new skills and start to use them on the job, then, and only then, may they be evaluated.

Training should be ongoing. As your program becomes a part of the company's process of doing business, it should be a regularly scheduled component of that process to train new personnel and to revitalize and update skills of longtime employees.

a. PREPARATION FOR TRAINING

1. Prepare a training plan

(a) Once you have completed your customer relations plan, go over it carefully to pinpoint areas where new employee skills are needed to make the plan work.

(b) All instruction should meet certain definite needs. Don't try to cover everything in one session.

(c) Decide who should receive the training. Only those needing the instruction should take part. We have conducted too many seminars where employees are there merely to pass the time for they will never be using the skills presented.

(d) Training should be introduced to employees as an opportunity, not as a reprimand or criticism of their performance or lack of skill.

2. Prepare a breakdown of the job or process

Whether you are conducting the training sessions yourself or using outside consultants, you need to have a clearly thought-out, logical method of instruction. If you are engaging consultants, check that they have a clearly planned curriculum, but one that is flexible enough to meet the changing needs of your business and your employees. Go over their material with them to see if their plans are well organized and if their methods and materials will meet the training objectives you have set.

(a) Training materials should concentrate on the important steps and key points to be learned.

(b) All steps or points should be clearly illustrated and demonstrated by the trainer.

(c) Details should be carefully selected and used only to emphasize and support the steps or points.

(d) Include any short cuts or knacks you can pass on that will help employees understand or perform new tasks or new skills.

3. Have everything ready for the training session

(a) Employees should know exactly what day, time, and place the training will take place. Make the training session important; give it meaning. People cannot do their jobs and attend a training session at the same time. Give them the time to attend, even if this means training at a hotel or training center.

(b) Keep numbers small so everyone can participate.

(c) The room, materials, and equipment should all be ready and functional before training begins. Poorly prepared instructors and equipment that doesn't work create a very poor impression.

(d) Start every session on time. This sets the tone for training and underlines its importance.

b. STEPS IN INSTRUCTING

1. Prepare the employee for instruction

(a) Put the employee at ease. In no way should employees feel they are being tested or reprimanded for poor performance.

We reiterate, training should be looked upon as a career opportunity to make work easier and more effective.

(b) Explain the training and its importance both to the employee and to the company. Explain its importance to the total customer relations plan.

(c) Create an interest. Employee involvement in creating the customer relations plan should have created interest in the training. Reinforce what the success of the total program will mean to the individual employee.

2. Present the training — show and tell

(a) The trainer should follow the sequence of the new task or the process.

(b) Explain or demonstrate one step at a time.

(c) Stress key points. How it is done, why it is done, why it should be done a certain way and not another. Don't waste time on unimportant details.

(d) Don't tell too much at one time. Stick to the facts. Repeat important points.

(e) Use simple language. Plain talk gets your message across best, but don't "talk down."

(f) Allow discussion.

(g) Allow participation — hands on rather than mere observation.

(h) Break into groups for problem solving and role playing. Employees can act the part of customers and experience situations from a different perspective.

(i) Set a high standard for the trainer's performance whether it is you or a consultant. If you are telling employees to be courteous and helpful to customers, but not demonstrating those qualities in your training sessions, your employees will react negatively. Trainers set the standard, not only for their own performances, but for that of the participants.

(j) Give reasons for methods and procedures. Rationale is important. The "why" and the "how" should be explained clearly.

(k) Show, demonstrate, teach one thing at a time. If part of your new customer relations plan is to create a customer mailing list, do not try to initiate this procedure with new employees until they have firmly grasped how to write the receipt, fill out a charge card slip, and handle returns. Add the new procedure once they have the routine of making the sale well in hand. A confused employee signals a confused business to a customer.

3. Try out the performance

(a) Have the employee do the job or follow the procedure. If possible have the employee do it in front of the full group or for a small group.

Whatever the method, make sure everyone involved in the training session gets to "do the job" during training. Praise and build confidence.

(b) Have the participants explain the key points of the job or procedures. This can be done while demonstrating in front of the total group or in small groups. This will assure you that the procedures and skills have been grasped by the participants.

4. Correcting errors or omissions

(a) Compliment before you correct.

(b) Do not belittle or be sarcastic.

(c) Build on the strengths shown by the participant.

(d) Let the participant correct himself or herself.

(e) If possible, do not correct in front of others. If you must, make the correction a general reminder for everyone.

(f) Don't be too quick to correct. The fault may lie with the trainer. Go over the information or procedure again for everyone's benefit.

5. Encourage participants

(a) Give sincere compliments.

(b) Thank them for good ideas.

(c) Be prompt with compliments.

6. Make sure participants have a complete understanding of the process, procedure, or skill

(a) If the employee seems to be slow in comprehension, arrange for individual consultation or more training.

7. Follow through

(a) Put the employees on their own when you feel they have the confidence and knowledge to complete the job, follow the procedure, or apply the new skills.

(b) Encourage more discussion and further questions — your door remains open.

(c) Check frequently, but gradually taper off as you see confidence growing and ability improving.

(d) Let employees know they are doing a good job. Your total customer relations plan has a method of measuring whether or not it is working. Newly acquired skills will either make the plan a success or failure. If there is need to further improve skills, say so. It is your responsibility to let employees know when they are doing a job correctly and also to let them know when improvement is called for.

(e) After a (designated) mutually agreed time, assess the total results of the training in respect to your customer relations program. Determine whether more training is necessary, if the principles need review, or if other employees should have similar training.

c. SUMMARY

Your new customer relations program may not work unless your employees receive some very specific training. Determine what that training should be, who should receive it, and who should teach it. Sell the training to your employees as an opportunity for growth for them and the organization. Training should not be seen as a punishment or criticism. Know exactly what it is you want the training to accomplish, what you want the participants to learn, and how they will apply those skills to their jobs. More important, show how the training will benefit your customer relations program over the long haul. Set aside time for the training. Create a learning environment. Keep the training procedures simple. Be sure everyone participates in the training and demonstrates their new skills or knowledge. Follow through. Skills need to be applied and then evaluated: Did the training have value? Did it make a difference to your customer relations success? And remember, training should produce living, breathing, thinking people who can function individually and pleasantly during the best of times, during depression, or during crisis.

CASE STUDY

Information from their customer surveys, the task forces, and staff discussion indicated that there was a need for training for the owners and employees of the ABC Shoppe. It was with a sense of anticipation that they all agreed to work on improving their personal skills. Areas for immediate attention included —

   (a) Sales training for everyone

   (b) Managerial skills for John

   (c) Interpersonal skills for April

   (d) Personal image help for June

11
TRAINING SPECIFICS

In chapter 10 we discussed the importance of training and how to set up a good training program. In this chapter we look at *specific* training that should be considered for your program.

Most businesses are set up like pyramids with management, considered the most important, at the top and service personnel and customers at the bottom.

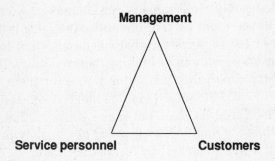

Management

Service personnel   Customers

Many training programs and reward systems concentrate on managers. By now, however, you must recognize that customers are the most important and should be at the top of the pyramid. Those who deal directly with customers, the service personnel, are next in importance and must be trained and rewarded accordingly.

Your pyramid should look like this:

Your frontline people are persuaders. They persuade customers to buy products, accept service, return again. Psychologists all agree that persuaders must have credibility if they are to persuade successfully. When your employees are knowledgeable, well-trained decision makers, your customers will see them as credible and have faith in them. Persuaders need to perceive what customers want to hear and need to know without destroying that credibility. Telling Mr. and Mrs. Smith that this is the house for them when financing it would threaten their personal economy and undermine their security does not make you a credible persuader. While the Smiths may love the house, they need to know what it will mean to their future debt load.

a. WHO TO TRAIN AND WHY

At the Disney theme parks, the employees who sweep the grounds and keep them spotlessly clean are given four days of intensive training. There is a 12-week turnover in these jobs as these are the people who are most likely to move into better jobs or who are working on school breaks. Why train them at all? The answer is, because guests at the theme park ask sweepers questions. Their responses can be the longest lasting memory of a Disney trip.

Who should be given specific training in customer service? Anyone who comes in contact with the public. American Express trains frontline people six to eight weeks; Proctor and Gamble's frontline staff are trained for three to five weeks before they take a customer phone order.

Included in your training program should be a recognition and reward system, the first step in your business recognition program. Learning new habits isn't always easy. Let your employees know they are doing well. A bottle of champagne, dinner for two, tickets to a show, or the parking spot of the month says, "well done," and makes the deserving trainee feel good about the training and its purpose.

b. HOW MUCH DO YOU KNOW ABOUT YOUR BUSINESS?

One of the expectations customers have is to do business with people who are knowledgeable about the company. Part of your training program should include —

- Company history and reputation
- What the company does — services, products
- Company organization
- Who does what within the organization
- Why the business works the way it does
- What common questions or problems arise
- Who has the answers to what
- Who has the authority for what decisions
- How the company ethics policy relates to customer service
- How each employee can be most effective

A lot of our consulting work is done within relatively large corporations. We are often surprised by how little one department knows about the function of another or about the company as a whole. Progressive companies recognize the value of knowing your product, which includes every aspect of the company. These companies have information-sharing sessions between departments, which helps to build a strong team.

c. WHAT DO YOU DO ON YOUR JOB?

One of the specifics to address in your training program is to determine how employees see their jobs. Have them write their own job descriptions during one of your training sessions — not the job descriptions that the company hired them under, but how they now perceive their jobs. If they describe their jobs as "answering the phones," "waiting on tables," "checking out purchases," without mention of helping customers meet their needs, you'll have to include some behavior modification in your training program so your employees will realize the value of good customer service. If someone does not like serving people, he or she should not be in customer-related position. Role play some actual situations to emphasize the following:

(a) Customers are people, not statistics, and should be treated with respect.

(b) Management trusts its frontline people.

(c) Management gives its frontline people the responsibility to solve customer problems, to have judgment and use it.

(d) Customers should come before the rules.

(e) Employees should fulfill the customers' needs.

(f) Giving service does not mean you are subservient. Be proud and professional about what you do. You want your employees to feel they have more at stake than just doing their job. By giving them personal power they will have confidence, seek information to do a better job, and have an attitude that results in positive behavior: I want to deal with customers and fulfill their wishes, not just put in my time so I can get on with my personal life.

d. EMPLOYEES' PERCEPTIONS OF THEMSELVES

Your training program should include videotaping role-playing situations that will allow employees to see and hear themselves as their customers do. A frequently quoted business study tells us we get our impressions of others through what we see, the tone of voice, and the words they use. What we see accounts for 55% of that impression. What we see includes clothing, grooming, posture, body language, gestures, and eye contact. The tone of voice accounts for 38% of the impression. Voices that are strident, nasal, harsh, flat, bored, lacking energy can make a very negative impression. That leaves only 7% for the actual words we say!

To demonstrate, use the following sentences two ways with an employee: "Boy, that was some job you did for us. I don't think I've seen anything like it before." The first time, be as disdainful as possible, let your body and voice reflect your exasperation and frustration. The employee won't feel very good about what you are saying! The next time, let your body, voice, and gestures reflect your pleasure and pride in the employee. The employee will respond in kind. Conclusion: you can say exactly the same words but your body and tone give very different messages.

Consider how important tone of voice is when customer contact is by telephone and there is no visual impression at all. The tone of the voice, plus the words, create for the customer a picture of the speaker on the other end who represents the business.

As employees watch the replays of their role-playing training situations, they will become acutely aware of how subtle changes to body language, tone of voice, and words can make gigantic changes to customer perception.

e. WHAT TRAINING SHOULD EMPHASIZE

Your training program should emphasize the following:

- The importance of a pleasant tone of voice
- The ability to control and modulate the voice under pressure
- Good manners and professional decorum
- Attention to detail
- The necessity to be systematic
- Good written communication skills (where applicable)
- Good verbal communication skills
- Above-average listening skills
- Good analytical skills

f. CHANGING OLD HABITS AND ADDING NEW ONES

Once a person is aware of a habit it can be changed if the person wishes to change it. Being made aware is the first step. That is why videotaping in training is such a good tool. In your training you can discover how many different ways you can say "May I help you?" Body language and tone of voice will convey a multitude of different messages from indifference to hostility! You will have some very specific new habits for your employees to practice, depending on the nature of your business. We will cover some pertinent to everyone in the business of giving customers service.

These are the most frequent customer service errors:

(a) *Saying,"I don't know."* It makes the customers lose confidence in the company. This habit can be changed with your training concerning company background. If the employee does not know, it is better to reply,"I don't have the answer right here. I'll

140

check and get back to you immediately. Sorry for the inconvenience."

(b) *Saying,"Hold on."* It's gruff and conveys impatience. New habit: "Please hold for a moment."

(c) *Saying,"You must," "You should" or "You have to."* Giving customers orders is counterproductive and can create animosity. New habit: "May I recommend" or "Two attractive options are," thereby allowing the customer to determine what to do.

(d) *Saying "Yeah" and "uh, uh" in response to a customer's "Thank you."* Both sound rough and uncaring. New habit: "yes" and "thank you." In some parts of the country you hear "youse" used as the plural for you as in "What would youse like for dessert?" This sounds very tough and uneducated. New habit: the plural for you is "you."

g. NEW HABITS — LISTENING SKILLS

Customers, as we said, expect to be heard. Although 75% of all we learn during our lifetime comes through speaking and listening, very few of us are trained in either. Listening should be part of your training program. Here are some basics to be considered in listening training. When dealing with customers, your employees should remember:

(a) Listening is not —

- "rest" before we start talking again,

- two narratives interrupting one another, or

- rattling off a list of questions or facts by rote.

(b) Good listening is —

- total concentration — hearing more than just words — taking in tone of voice, facial and body expression, even breathing,

- listening with sensitivity,

- responding directly to what has been said which inspires the speaker to speak with greater clarity and eloquence,

- active and supportive — you must want to listen because you are interested in what the speaker has to say, and

- listening to what is being said NOW. Don't anticipate your next question.

(c) Good listeners never —

- assume — they get the facts. (Remember, when you assume, you make an ass of you and me!)

- cut off the listening by taking what is being said personally,

- think they know it all,

- talk too much (they let the customer talk), or

- give too much information (keep your responses simple).

(d) Positive listening habits include —

- getting rid of external distractions. Take the customer away from other conversation. Find a private place if necessary where you won't be interrupted.

- dealing with your own emotions, attitudes, biases, opinions, and prejudices that could keep you from listening

- not faking interest. Your glazed or wandering eyes will give you away.

- giving time to the speaker but being prepared to move the dialogue along by asking pertinent questions.

(e) Training should emphasize active listening and response, including —

- strong eye contact,

- lively facial expression,

- vital body language,

- verbal attends, "Yes," "I see," "Go on,"

- door opener questions so the customer will talk, "who, what, where, how, when, why,"

- reflecting back what you see and hear, including restating content or feelings and restating to give confirmation,

- stating the main point that needs to be resolved,

- declaring your action of what will be done,

- taking action,

- confirming results, and

- evaluating results.

h. NEW HABITS — BUILDING CUSTOMER COMMUNICATION SKILLS

People buy (things, ideas, projects) from people who are most like them. To improve communication with your customer, you can learn to identify his or her communication style and then adapt to it.

1. Preferred communication styles

Everyone has a favorite way of accessing information. Some people understand what they see better than what they hear or feel. Such people rely on a *visual* communication style. Other people depend on what they hear. This group of people uses and responds to an *auditory* style of communication. A third method of communication depends on "gut reaction" — good rapport is the most important element of comunication for those who rely on *feeling*.

The following chart shown as Figure #3 will help you recognize characteristics common to these three styles of communication.

Identifying the communication style of your customer will help you know how to approach him or her.

2. Mirror the communicator

One way to adapt to the customer is to mirror his or her communication style.

(a) Mirror body language and posture very subtly. If the other person is very laid back, you don't want to appear overly aggressive. Relax a bit. If the other person is aggressive, don't let him or her overpower you. Give your body more vitality, the spine a bit more starch.

(b) Mirror the speech pattern. If the speaker has a slow delivery while you are a rapid talker, slow down a bit. If you are naturally slow in delivery, increase your rate slightly with someone who speaks quickly.

(c) If someone is angry or agitated you don't want to mirror his or her emotions, but you do want to mirror the intensity of his or her emotions through emphatic words and the strength of the voice.

When mirroring, be very careful that you are not perceived as mimicking or being condescending. If you wish to influence the communicator's style, first mirror the speaker, then gradually shift to the style you want to create. The other person may well mirror you!

3. Adapt to communication styles

(a) Match their language. Use their words. To the visual say, "I see what you mean." To the auditory, "I hear what you say." To the feeling, "I feel the same way."

(b) Accept their eye movement. Don't perceive downward glances as being shifty or evasive.

FIGURE #3
STYLES OF COMMUNICATION

	VISUAL	AUDITORY	FEELING
ACTIONS	Needs to make eye contact. Makes "to do" lists. Uses hands when speaking.	No need for eye contact. Remembers — no list. Can do other things while listening or speaking.	Learns by doing. Draws diagrams while speaking. Needs to touch or nudge.
LANGUAGE	Look, see, picture, view, notice, "See you tomorrow."	Hear, say, tell, sounds, listen, "Talk to you tomorrow."	Grasp, excite, understand, feel, touch, "I'll be in touch."
EYE MOVEMENT	Looks upward when listening.	Looks to left or right or down and to the left.	Looks down and to the right.
PROBLEMS	Wants people to "pay attention" and make eye contact when they are speaking or listening.	May appear to not be "paying attention." Very frustrating for others.	Must realize that people may not want to be touched and won't be able "to hear" until they are away from the toucher.

(c) Adapt your eye movement. Make eye contact with a visual person even though you may be an auditory communicator.

By adapting, you make the speaker/listener believe you are giving greater attention to the communication.

i. NEW HABITS — WORDS THAT WORK

We said that words account for only 7% of the impression that is made on others. Therefore, it is important that your training emphasize words that make the strongest, most positive impression. Some of these are:

- "What can I do to help you fulfill (or satisfy) your needs?" (Too long? Try, "How may I help you?")

- "We...." It tells customers there is a team working on their behalf.

- "Thank you."

- "I don't have the answer, but I will get that information for you."

- "We made a mistake. What can I do to correct it?"

- "Your idea is better than mine."

- "Let's work together."

- "What do you think?"

- "Appreciate," as in "I really appreciate your calling to tell us..."

- "Concerned," as in "I am very concerned about your complaint."

Your training should also emphasize eliminating words that do not work and that create a negative impression. Some of these are —

- "Never," as in "We never sell items out of the window display."

146

- "That's not the way we do it here."

- "You must be mistaken."

- "Company policy...."

- "We've always done...."

- "We would never have promised you that."

- "What else can I tell you?"

- "What else do you expect?"

- "It's not my job."

- "We're not responsible."

- "I can only do one thing at a time."

- "Just calm down."

j. NEW HABITS — TELEPHONE TECHNIQUES

As we mentioned before, the tone of voice and the words are extremely important when sales and service are conducted by the phone. Your telephone training should include the following:

- How to keep a pleasant tone in the voice at all times. (Mirrors help! See yourself smile before you talk. Hang up your bad mood with your coat.)

- Saying the name of the company clearly.

- Starting with a warm welcome.

- Establishing control — "What can I do for you?"

- Restating at the conclusion of the conversation, particularly if you have talked for any length of time

- Bringing the conversation to a close by asking,"Is there anything else I can do for you?" (The answer is either yes or no.)"What else can I do for you?" is open-ended and invites more general talk.

- Knowing what to do if you need to look up information. (Say, "Please call me back at 1 p.m." or "Mr. Smith, I'll have that information after 1 p.m. When may I call you back? If you are not in, is there someone else I can leave the information with?")

- Having all information at hand when calling.

- Taking names. When taking a name, have the person spell it for you. In brackets, spell it phonetically or make pronunciation notes so you will be able to say it later. For instance, for the name "Guidense" you might write "guy-den-say" or "gee-denz."

- Using the caller's name, formally, immediately to reinforce it. ("Yes, Mrs. Dunckel, we do have that model in stock.")

- Making the caller feel important.

- Ensuring that you do not waste your time or the caller's time.

- Learning all the technical techniques of transferring and logging calls.

- Adapting to the company's policy of answering the phone and identifying yourself and the department.

- Learning the techniques of feedback, paraphrasing, and restatement.

k. HOW TO REMEMBER CUSTOMER NAMES

Recognizing, acknowledging, and serving repeat customers establishes a strong bond of loyalty. Your specific training program may include instruction in how to remember customers and use their names:

(a) Time: Take time to look directly at the customer so you can remember what he or she looks like. Smile and make eye contact.

(b) Prepare: Be ready to listen. Don't let your mind wander to the fact that the customer looks like Uncle Harry or wears a toupee!

(c) Focus: Concentrate on the customer and what is being said.

(d) Attend: Pay attention to the customer's name.

(e) Repeat: Repeat the customer's name immediately, spell it out, write it down, pronounce it. It may help to remember that it rhymes with another word (Dunckel rhymes with uncle.) It may help to visualize. (If the name is Taylor, visualize the customer measuring and sewing).

(f) Remark: Make an appropriate remark using the customer's name. "I recognize your name from our customer list, Mr. Johnson."

(g) Use: Use the customer's name several times, but don't overuse and call attention to what you are doing.

(h) Part: Use the customer's full name when he or she departs. "The delivery will be made Tuesday. Thank you for your order, Mr. Johnson."

(i) Recall: At the end of the day, visualize the customers you served.

(j) Attach: Connect the customer's name to your visualization. If necessary refer to your written note, credit card receipt, or bill.

(k) Reuse: Use the customer's name again the next time you see him or her. "It's Mr. Johnson, isn't it?" If it isn't — start all over again.

1. NEW HABITS — DEALING WITH MORE THAN ONE CUSTOMER AT A TIME

Customers expect recognition. Recognition can be established immediately through eye contact, a smile, and a greeting. If an employee is serving a customer, an "I'll be with you in a moment" with a smile recognizes the existence of the other customer and the assurance that he or she will be taken care of. Your training should include situations that emphasize this good habit. Include telephone interruptions in your role-playing scenarios. The following points should be included in your training:

(a) Don't scatter your attention. Acknowledge the new customer, then focus your attention on the person you are serving.

(b) Be sure to acknowledge others. All others. If there are several people waiting to be served, smile, take them all in and say, "I'll be serving you in turn in just a moment."

(c) The person you are serving deserves your attention. If a call comes in, take it, "Right now I have customer at the counter, may I take your name and number and call you back in 15 minutes?" Then apologize to the person waiting at the counter. Be sure to call back.

m. NEW HABITS — DEALING WITH THE CUSTOMER WHO DOESN'T SPEAK ENGLISH

If many of your customers are new citizens, you may consider some special training for employees. Your training sessions may include the following ideas:

(a) Learn a few phrases of the language spoken by your customers.

(b) Identify those among your staff who speak other languages and could be called upon to act as interpreters. Names can be put on an easily accessed card for quick referral.

(c) Practice slowing down your speech and not speaking louder.

(d) Learn to get the customer's name and use it: "Mr. Poon, I appreciate that you speak more than one language, but, unfortunately, I only speak English. I want to help you..." If you are face to face, get the customer to write out his or her name and request. The written word is unaccented!

n. DEALING WITH LEGITIMATE COMPLAINTS

As hard as you try, things can go wrong and customers can have very legitimate complaints which should be dealt with accordingly. Complaints usually fall into five categories. Your training program should emphasize how to solve them.

Problem: Didn't get what was promised.

Solution: Apologize, rectify, follow up to see that the customer is satisfied.

Problem: Someone was rude on the phone or in person.

Solution: Apologize. Assure it won't happen again. Then investigate the employee who was reported to be rude. Attitude or vocal tone may be the fault and should be rectified.

Problem: No one went out of the way to provide service. The customer was not acknowledged and was treated with indifference.

Solution: Too often customers in this situation will not complain. They just will not return. This problem should not be allowed to exist. The solution is the same as the second problem above.

Problem: Nobody listened to their problem.

Solution: Same as problem three.

Problem: A company person was negative.

*Solution:*Same as problem two. If employees do not have the attitude that the customer is number one, they should not be in the service industry.

None of these situations should be allowed to happen, but when they do, how your employees handle them is vital to ongoing customer relations, for if the complaint is handled satisfactorily, the customer will return.

Even if you've had a bad experience with a customer you must remain unbiased. To label them as "turkeys" or deadbeats or to think, "Here we go again," "Not again" or "We can never do right for them," will be reflected in your body language and vocal tone. Ninety percent of all customers are decent, rational people. The ones you see, hear, and remember are the difficult 10%. While much of your training is directed toward that 10%, don't neglect the 90%.

Here are the steps to follow in handling legitimate complaints:

(a) Give your name and personal commitment to solving the problem.

(b) Apologize. Make no excuses.

(c) Ask questions. Get all the details of the complaint. Answering questions allows the customer to vent feelings and allows you to get the information needed to make a decision.

(d) Write the complaint down. Writing it down gives the complaint importance and permanence for follow-up.

(e) Read it back to the customer. This action assures clarification and mutual understanding. In very serious situations, you may ask him or her to initial the written complaint.

(f) Deal with each point of the complaint individually. This action whittles the problem down to a size that is easy to solve.

(g) If the problem has to be left with you to be solved, get back to the customer and report what has been done.

(h) Follow up after the problem has been solved. "How are we doing now?" This may be done by phone or a hand-written note.

o. DEALING WITH DIFFICULT CUSTOMERS

Customer relations would be easy if all customers were satisfied by quality service and all employees were caring and responsible. Unfortunately, not all customers are happy even when employees are giving quality products and service.

Your training in dealing with difficult customers should outline the same steps as discussed for legitimate complaints, but should also stress that when emotions are involved, the customer needs special care.

1. Employee reaction

It is only natural to respond emotionally to emotion. When this happens we become defensive. Employees are apt to say, "I didn't take your order" or they may blame someone else in an attempt to deflect blame, "Mary must have taken your order."

Customers don't care who did it, they just want action. The employee may lay blame on the system, "We've been having a problem with our computers." Again, the customer doesn't care why it happened, only how it is going to be resolved.

2. Logical employee vs. emotional customer

Your training program should emphasize that emotional customers will not respond initially to logic. That is why they must deal with those emotions first.

Employee	Angry customer
Both sides of the brain functioning. Is logical, factual, calm.	Only right side of the brain functioning. Is emotional, doesn't hear. Doesn't respond to logic.
Voice is quiet, low-pitched, slow paced.	Voice is loud, high-pitched, incoherent, stammering, even profane.

Be warned that, if the employee cannot calm the customer and bring him or her over to logical thinking, the employee may be dragged over to the emotional side and you will have two emotional people who are loud, not listening, incoherent etc.

3. Training for dealing with the emotional customer

Employees should be trained so that they will —

(a) not rush to solve the problem. They should deal with the customer's feelings and emotions first and deal with the problem second.

(b) not take what is said personally. They must separate their personal selves from their business selves; otherwise they will react with personal emotion.

(c) remain calm when confronted by an emotional customer.

Inside, Eddie Employee is reacting with, "I don't have to take this," "Who is he to talk to me like that?" The danger is that he will verbalize this "self-talk." Encourage him to change his self-talk to, "Keep calm," "Listen," "Breath." Eddie should calmly assure the customer that he, the customer, and the company are all against the problem and can solve it together.

4. Communicating with difficult or angry customers

Customer problems cannot be solved without communication. Your training should emphasize the various types of complainer and how to communicate with each.

(a) Communicating with the unresponsive person

When someone has little to say, ask questions that need to be answered with full sentences and disclosure:

- What is the problem?
- How did that happen?
- What can my department do to help you?
- What can I do?

If you need more information, cut in with the short questions:

- How so?
- Who?
- Why?

(b) Communicating with the whiner

Whiners like to talk about their feelings, their hurts, and their disappointments. You need to get them to "action" communication. Ask questions like:

- How could it have been done better?
- What do you want to happen in the future?

(c) Communicating with the person whose anger is controlled

When people keep their anger bottled up, you cannot communicate with them. The words may not indicate their mood, but their tone of voice will. Think of the world of meaning contained in the word "nothing" said in response to, "What's bothering you, dear?" You've got to get the anger expressed before you can communicate.

- Express what you see. "You are obviously concerned about this." "You have every right to be upset."

- Get them to talk. "How did you feel when...?" "What was your reaction to...?"

- Once they have expressed their anger, move on to action questions. "What do we need to do...?"

5. Communicating with rude customers

Your training should also consider rude customers or customers bent on embarrassing someone:

- Keep cool

- Smile and ask "What would you like me to do to solve this problem?" or "I'm having a problem meeting your expectations. What can I do?"

6. Communicating with the hostile person

You cannot communicate with someone who is shouting.

- Let them shout. They need to diffuse their anger.

- Listen actively.

- Use non-verbal skills such as eye contact and nods, lean toward the speaker, and maintain a concerned facial expression

- Use verbal skills such as "Yes, I see"

- Ask questions that allow them to talk.

- Restate their feelings and the main points that are making them angry.

- Choose the main point that needs to be resolved.

- Restatement gives confirmation of your attention to their concern.

- Move to action questions: "What can be done to rectify this situation?"

When dealing with an emotional customer you will be in charge if you:

- Lower the pitch of your voice

- Talk more slowly.

- Make strong eye contact.

- Tell the customer what you can do — not what you can't do.

- Use silence. If you say nothing, you will not respond to the negatives of the customer. It gives you time to think. Keep a non-threatening gaze and an interested, concerned facial expression.

- Agree to disagree. Refuse to argue. Repeat the customer's opinion. Restate the facts and what can be done.

7. Communicating with customers who are drunk or using profanities

Your business should have a policy regarding how an employee handles a customer who is drunk or using profanities. How to implement the policy should be part of your customer training program. No employee should be verbally abused by anyone, nor should they be placed in a position of potential danger.

What to say to abusive customers? Try saying, "I'm sorry *(name of customer if you know it)*, but if you cannot speak on a professional basis, I'll have to *(call my manager, call security, terminate this call)*." Record all information about the encounter immediately following. If it was witnessed by another employee, have him or her read and sign your notes. When people get very emotional they often cannot remember exactly what they said or whether they were the ones who said it.

157

p. CUSTOMER RELATIONS PROCEDURE MANUALS

Whatever procedures you develop for your training program should be set out in an employee customer relations procedure manual. Service standards decline if they are not —

- written down
- clear and specific
- monitored
- equally enforced

In determining what should go into your manual, you should remember that customer service is based on your business's needs and goals, but more important, on your customer's needs and wants.

Manuals should cover everything pertaining to a customer encounter: verbal communication, written communication, shipping, delivery, etc.

1. Manual contents

Your manual should specify clearly the steps to be taken for every customer encounter. Use a bullet form format which can be referred to quickly and read easily. For example, your manual may include the steps to be taken when answering the telephone.

The procedure may cover such points as:

- How many times the phone can ring before it must be answered.
- How the employee identifies the company, the department, and himself or herself.
- Whether notes should be taken, and how.
- How to answer questions.
- How to answer hostile or difficult questions.
- How to transfer calls.

- Whether callers should be put on hold, and how.
- How to close the call.

Examples may be included to act as a guide: "Good afternoon, this is the order department, April Jones speaking. How may I help you?"

2. Manual format

Set up your manual so that it is easy to use, read, and add to.

- Print pages on one side only.
- Use a three-ring binder.
- Use an expandable number system that allows for additions as your customer service program grows and changes. Your pages may start numbered 1, 2, 3, but you may end up with pages 1, 1a, 2, 2a, 2b, 3.

If your manual has few pages and your employees work with it frequently, you may wish to laminate the pages for cleanliness and durability.

q. SUMMARY

Good customer relations are very fragile and can be severed by one unthinking, untrained employee. Your training program should deal with specifics that will assure repeat business through service excellence.

(a) Training should recognize the individual employee's strengths and correct his or her weaknesses.

(b) Old habits should be replaced by new that will make both the employee and the customer feel good about themselves.

(c) Training should give frontline people the knowledge and power to act.

(d) Training should feature role-playing sessions that cover real life situations. Discussion should follow. Videotaping should be used if possible.

(e) Training should emphasize how to deal with complaints immediately, efficiently, to the customer's satisfaction, and, if possible, by the person who served the customer initially.

(f) Make training skills an ongoing procedure with easy-to-follow company policy manuals.

CASE STUDY

It had become clear that the employees of the ABC Shoppe needed some specific training. A weekend sales training program was offered by a consulting company with a sound international reputation. John and Mary made an executive decision, and with a couple of weeks' notice to the public, closed the store for the weekend. They subsequently agreed the loss in revenue was compensated by the gain in knowledge. They were able to monitor the success of the training by implementing the skills learned and the results that followed. Even more rewarding, they found their customers favorable to the idea of personnel training.

John was able to get his managerial training one evening a week over a two-month period at the local community college. He shared his enthusiasm for his new-found knowledge with Mary and the rest of the staff at their weekly meeting.

Not wanting to isolate April, Jim and June joined her one evening a week at the community college for a course on interpersonal skills. All three found the course rewarding. Jim became less brusque and his attitude mellowed; June tempered her bubbly outbursts and channeled her natural enthusiasm toward getting the customer enthused. And, most important, April discovered the image she projected to the world was a facade to make up for what she felt were her inadequacies.

Videotaped role playing showed the differences between a smile and a frown, the tone and influence of the voice, the

160

overuse of slang and negative body language. Jim, June, and April became very supportive of each other and the team spirit was encouraged by John and Mary.

Finally, one store meeting focussed on personal image — what would best reflect the store's image of quality and prestige. Mary arranged for a friend who was an image and color consultant to speak informally. She also arranged for personal consultation for each staff member and herself. The result was that the entire staff benefited. Mary, April, and June spent an evening in a quality consignment store putting together a "store wardrobe" for June. The cost was less than one-third of what it would have cost originally. The basic four pieces, two blouses, and two skirts translated into four different outfits, or eight when accessorized. June stayed within her limited budget while the quality image of the store's sales staff remained consistent.

Your business will have very different skills to be learned depending on the products and service you supply. Customer relations goes beyond the job skills of working on the production line, repairing the car engine, keeping the books. Customer relations training is training employees to give customers what they want, when they want it, and how they want it.

12

BRINGING IT ALL TOGETHER

Now that you have read through the preceding chapters, here is a quick review.

a. THE CUSTOMER RELATIONS PROGRAM

Figure #4 on the next page shows the steps in a successful customer relations program:

(a) Research: What is your image as perceived by yourself? Your image as perceived by customers?

(b) Set goals: What do you want your image and reputation to be?

(c) Implement procedures: Take steps to make goals a reality.

(d) Monitor: Set in place methods to determine whether steps are being followed.

(e) Evaluate: Determine if the procedures are getting the results to achieve your goals.

(f) Adjust: Be prepared to make changes.

(h) Communication and training: Ongoing at every step of the process.

b. DESIGNING YOUR CRITICAL PATH

1. Do your research

(a) Identify the image of your business at the present time as perceived by you, your people, and your customers. This can be done with questionnaires,

162

FIGURE #4
STEPS IN A CUSTOMER RELATIONS PROGRAM

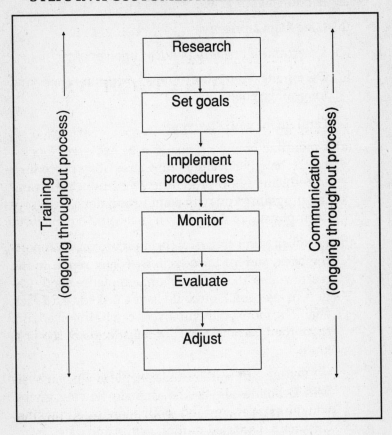

meetings, one-on-one conversations, and telephone calls. Make sure everyone is asked the same questions so that you are able to use and compare fairly the information received.

(b) Determine what you want the image of your business to be.

(c) Determine what must be changed, compromised, or added to turn that image into a reality.

2. Set goals for your business

(a) Set down your goals.

(b) Give them a priority.

(c) Determine if one is dependent upon another.

(d) Determine your short-range, medium-range, and long-range goals.

3. Implement your strategy

(a) Determine how each goal can be achieved. Does it mean changing or eliminating an existing procedure, introducing a new procedure, or introducing a training program? You may want to appoint a task force of employees to study how a goal could be achieved.

(b) Establish a time frame for their discussion, for reporting back, and for introduction of their report to the rest of your staff for discussion, acceptance, modification, or rejection. You could have a task force for each goal. The more your employees can be involved, the more they become a part of the success of the program.

Setting a time frame tells people you mean business. Deadlines also get the adrenalin flowing, giving you the extra energy and motivation to get cracking. Chapter 8 discussed putting names and dates to actions that need to take place; when all task force members have a current flowchart that specifies people, places, and progress it's surprising how well people respond to their responsibilities.

There must be no surprises. Everybody must be kept up to date. It takes only one employee to sarcastically ask, "They're doing *what* today?" to cast doubt on the veracity of the program. If the program has been well planned and if everybody has been kept informed, a launch date will create excitement and anticipation as your business "family" eagerly awaits the birth of the latest offspring.

4. Monitor progress and success

Once you have established the methods needed to reach your goals, you must establish a way to monitor the progress and success of each goal. This method could be determined by the task force that established the program for achievement, or it could evolve from employee discussion following the agreement on procedure. Whatever the method, it must be acceptable to the employees.

You may consider customer surveys through questionnaires or telephone interviews, monitoring of employees' performance through an agreed upon procedure, or feedback from employees at regularly designated intervals.

The program must be monitored at the times and dates agreed upon. Delay leads to further delay and frustration for those who are keeping their part of the bargain. Timely monitoring prevents problems festering from neglect and will send a signal to your customers that you mean what you say.

Timely monitoring will also encourage prompt adjustments and necessary changes. The longer a problem prevails, the harder it becomes to change or improve it; it becomes entrenched.

5. Evaluate

Assess your program. Have you achieved the goals you established?

This is where you bring it all together and see if your bottom line makes sense. Sample #8 at the end of this chapter will help you do this. Alternatively, you may wish to design your own chart for measuring your program's success.

Now answer these questions:

(a) Have overall sales increased above traditional or seasonal growth?

(b) Have profits increased?

(c) Has the regular customer base increased?

(d) Has the regular customer base increased its buying?

(e) Has the number of new customers increased?

(f) Have new customers become repeats?

(g) Are satisfied customers referring others?

(h) Has the employee base increased or decreased? (If it has decreased, is your operation more efficient? If it has increased, has it been to provide better service?)

(i) Have employee resignations increased or decreased?

(j) Has the program given employees pride and recognition?

(k) Has the cost of training been defrayed by an increase in revenue or has it not been justified?

6. Adjust

Be ready to change some goals and set some new ones if necessary. There's no disgrace in admitting an idea didn't work; in fact it's a sign of maturity and business acumen to recognize a problem early and correct it before damage can ensue. After all, isn't business all about profiting from our mistakes?

CASE STUDY

This is a good point at which to summarize the study of the ABC Shoppe. Over a period of six months, the store increased both its client base and its sales. Profits went up 23%. John and Mary found that 46% of their increase in sales could be traced directly to repeat customers. They also discovered that 35% of their new customers were direct referrals from satisfied customers. They had no resignations, although they realized they would soon have to replace June who would be graduating from university in six months. But they had a bonus because she agreed to help them find her own replacement when the time came. As she said, she didn't want just anyone working in "her store."

The cost for training was under $2,000. John and Mary agreed that $2,000 a year seemed a small sum to pay to keep profits climbing, customers satisfied, staff up to date, and to maintain unlimited potential for continued growth and success.

SAMPLE #8
"THE BOTTOM LINE"

	Average at start of program	3 mos. later	6 mos. later	1 yr. later	% overhead
Revenue					
Profit					
Customer base					
Repeat customer base					
New customers					
Repeat of new customers					
Customers referred by customers					
Employee base					
Employee resignations					
Cost of training					